OXFORD
UNIVERSITY PRESS

Blackstone's Police Investigators'
Mock Examination Paper 2019

Pack 1

Contents

OXFORD
UNIVERSITY PRESS

Great Clarendon Street, Oxford, OX2 6DP,
United Kingdom

Oxford University Press is a department of the University of Oxford.
It furthers the University's objective of excellence in research, scholarship,
and education by publishing worldwide. Oxford is a registered trade mark of
Oxford University Press in the UK and in certain other countries

© David Pinfield and Paul Connor 2018

The moral rights of the authors have been asserted

First Edition published in 2004
Fifteenth Edition published in 2018
Impression: 3

Crown copyright material is reproduced under Class Licence
Number C01P0000148 with the permission of OPSI
and the Queen's Printer for Scotland

Published in the United States of America by Oxford University Press
198 Madison Avenue, New York, NY 10016, United States of America

British Library Cataloguing in Publication Data

Data available

ISBN 978–0–19–883137–2

Printed in Great Britain by Bell & Bain Ltd., Glasgow

Acknowledgements

Thanks to all the staff at Oxford University Press, particularly Peter Daniell and Amy Baker. I would like to thank Jenny, my daughter, for assistance with proofreading this publication. I also very much appreciate the support over the years of my friend, Darryl Winn, and that of my wife, Diane, who has helped in the logistics of this product.

Dave Pinfield

Introduction to the Mock Examination

Many students embarking on the National Investigators' Examination (NIE) have not sat a formal examination of this type, albeit a number will have had the experience of the Sergeants' and/or Inspectors' promotion examination. The preparation for the NIE is daunting as it involves having to study in excess of 500 pages of text in a 14-week time frame; this is far more intense than either the Sergeants' or Inspectors' examinations.

To assist your preparation you can obtain multiple-choice questions (MCQs) from a variety of different sources. The Blackstone's online MCQ database is an excellent resource and is available via Oxford University Press. It contains a growing database of multiple-choice questions, based directly on the content of the *Blackstone's Police Investigators' Manual*, and you can find more information here: http://www.blackstonespoliceservice.com/. The *Blackstone's Police Investigators' Q&A 2019* is also available and contains in excess of 300 questions specifically designed for the NIE student. But whilst these are very useful to assist in testing your knowledge, they do not do so in the same way you will be tested in the NIE—this mock examination will. Whilst it is impossible to recreate the exact same MCQs you will face in the exam or to mirror the pressure you will naturally feel, taking this mock is an extremely useful exercise—for example:

- How is your time management?
- What does it feel like to sit an 80 MCQ examination?
- Do you have unidentified weaknesses in your knowledge?

This mock exam can help you find answers to those questions.

To make this experience as relevant as possible you need to consider that the examination contains 80 MCQs, 10 of which are 'validation' MCQs. 'Validation' MCQs are effectively 'test' questions—if they perform well enough, they will be introduced to future exams as 'counting' MCQs. So you are actually marked out of 70.

The MCQs in your examination are taken from the *Blackstone's Investigators' Manual 2019* and the four sections it contains (General Principles, Police Powers and Procedures; Serious Crime and Other Offences; Property Offences; and Sexual Offences).

If we look at the feedback from the last 54 examinations we can see that the average NIE consists of 27 MCQs on General Principles, Police Powers and Procedures, 16 MCQs on Serious Crime and Other Offences, 16 MCQs on Property Offences and 11 on Sexual Offences (the 70 MCQs that count towards your mark)—so your mock will more or less mirror that structure (and include 10 MCQs that, for marking purposes, will be considered as 'validation' MCQs). As in your NIE, to pass you will need to answer correctly 39 out of 70 questions (55.71%).

You have two hours to complete the examination at an examination centre (giving you 90 seconds per question). The examination usually takes place the first Tuesday of either March, June, September, or the end of November, but this is subject to change. You will need to arrive at the examination centre 30 minutes before the examination starts. To date this has always been 1.30 pm for arrival at the test centre and 2.00 pm for commencement of the examination. Failure to be there at the allotted time will prevent you taking the examination.

The format and rules of the NIE are exactly the same as for the Sergeants' and Inspectors' examination, and there are many instances of candidates who have been delayed not being allowed to enter the examination room. You will be working hard to prepare for this examination: DO NOT put yourself under pressure by running late on the day of the examination. To gain entry to the examination centre you need to hand in a pink registration form (sent to your force) and show your warrant card. Your mobile phone has to be left in a receptacle at the rear of the examination room as modern technology could allow you to photograph or send a text after the examination begins, to assist a colleague. You will not be allowed to leave in the first or last half-hour of the examination. All examination centres across the country start the examination at the same time. There is a senior invigilator who will read out all the rules relating to the examination: listen carefully to them. Examples of possible reasons why you could be removed from the examination include opening the exam paper before being told to do so or omitting to hand in your mobile phone. There will be other invigilators at the centre to assist in setting up the room and to ensure that everyone abides by the rules. If you wish to leave the room to go to the toilet you will be escorted there and back by an invigilator of the same sex.

Some of the questions are shorter than others. Each question contains a story or account, known as the 'stem'. A 'lead-in' follows: this is the question. Then you will be required to select an answer from the four possible answers, marked A, B, C and D. Multiple-choice questions using roman numerals as answer options are NOT contained in this examination, for example:

A (i) and (ii).
B (ii) and (iii).
C (ii) only.
D (iii) only.

You will find that on occasions the question will seem very easy and, through your revision, you will be able to identify the correct answer almost immediately. This mental effect will give you confidence for the next question. On other occasions, you will see a question and be able to narrow it down to two options. Some students will be of the belief that the two examples they have ruled out are stupid or ridiculous. This is not the case: it is knowledge that you have which has allowed you to make that decision. Question writers will give four viable options, only one of which will be the right answer. For example, see the following:

Pasta Carbonara is a famous Italian dish which you will have all probably eaten either at home or at a restaurant. In the original Italian recipe what is the main base of the sauce?

A Eggs.
B Cheese.
C Cream.
D Olive oil.

The correct answer is A; you may have realised that it was not either cheese or olive oil whether it was prepared at home or eaten in a restaurant; however, many of the sauces in supermarkets and less authentic restaurants tend to use a cream sauce but the real carbonara sauce is egg-based.

Now for a question where many of you will have less knowledge.

Where in the human body are the Islets of Langerhans?

   A The inner ear.
   B The brain cortex.
   C The pancreas.
   D The spine.

Answer C. How many of you were correct on this one? Unless you have studied biology or suffer with diabetes you are unlikely to know. Do not waste time on this sort of question if you have no idea of the correct answer, as there will be no divine inspiration; select and move on. There will be long questions that need time for you to comprehend fully what is being asked so do not waste time on something you do not know. That is not to devalue any question, whether it is hard, easy, or in between; they all have a value of 1.42% towards your end result.

All the questions in this mock examination are written not only to test you but also to prepare you for the examination. In the actual NIE the answer sheet is smaller than the one provided here and it could be easy to make a mistake. Do not decide to miss a question with a view to returning to it later as if under pressure you forget, all your answers could be one out. For example, if you miss out question 36 because you do not know the answer, and move on to question 37, you could easily put the answer to question 37 in the blank row for question 36 in error. I can assure you that I have had at least one student where I am convinced from their result, and knowing the hard work they have put in, that their result was an admin failure.

An optical reader reads the answer sheet: it picks up the pencil marks on your sheet. Therefore, if you have answered B and then rub it out and put D, but have not fully erased the incorrect option, it will void this as it will show two answers. So, if you wish to mark anything to remind yourself later, use the question paper NOT the answer sheet, as even pencil marks outside the marking matrix will void the question. If you do have to erase an answer, ensure you do it with care.

All the very best in this examination: luck should not be required.

Dave Pinfield

Instructions for Completion

READ THE WHOLE OF THE INSTRUCTIONS BEFORE ATTEMPTING THE MOCK EXAMINATION

If you want to get the most from this mock examination then you must treat it as if you were sitting the examination proper.

Time

You have up to two hours to complete the examination. It might not take you that long but it is best to assume that it will, so please make absolutely sure that you set aside two hours. You cannot expect to sit part of the examination for one hour, take a break for 20 minutes, return to the examination and then get an accurate picture of your performance. The examination must be completed in one two-hour sitting. If you want to, why not try and complete the examination between 14.00 hours and 16.00 hours, as this is the time period you will sit the examination proper in 2019? You should have been told by your respective police force that the pass mark is 55% (55.71% exact).

Environment

You need to be able to concentrate on the examination and you cannot do that if the television is on, the phone is ringing, etc. Find a place where you will not be disturbed for the two hours this examination will take and make sure that there are no distractions that will affect your performance.

Equipment

Ideally, you will sit at a single desk to take the examination, but I appreciate that in most cases this will not be possible. However, you will need a table and chair of some description. Trying to fill out the answer sheet on your lap whilst holding the question paper open will prove to be a difficult task to say the least.

Make sure that you can see a clock, stopwatch, or wristwatch. It would be best to have two timepieces, just in case one stops.

You will need two pencils, a pencil sharpener, and an eraser.

Pack 1

In Pack 1 you will find a blank answer sheet and the question booklet. Place both documents on the table.

When you decide to start the examination, please open the question booklet. Work through the test questions and make your choice of A, B, C or D by putting a horizontal line through the corresponding letter on the answer sheet.

Do not make any notes or doodles on the answer sheet. If you wish to make any marks, do so on the question booklet.

Mark only one answer for each question. If two or more choices are made then the question would be marked as incorrect in the examination proper.

Make sure that if you change your answer you erase the previous mark fully.

If you leave an answer blank then it would be marked incorrect in the examination proper. Try not to leave blank answers when you are unsure. Mark an answer and come back to the question if you have time at the end of the examination.

Pack 2

When you have finished the examination, open Pack 2 and begin the marking process. When you have finished marking your paper, please refer to the answer booklet for a detailed explanation of the correct answers with paragraph references to the *Blackstone's Police Investigators' Manual 2019*.

The marking process will take some time—to ensure accuracy; please do not rush this stage!

OXFORD
UNIVERSITY PRESS

Blackstone's Police Investigators'
Mock Examination Paper 2019

Question Booklet

Time Allowed—120 minutes

1. Each of the questions is followed by four possible answers, only ONE of which is correct. Choose the ONE response that you consider to be correct. On the answer sheet mark the box that corresponds to your selection. Mark your answer clearly with a — mark. The answer sheet has spaces for your answers to all questions. If you change your mind about an answer, rub out the first mark, then mark your new answer. Mark only one answer for each question.

2. You are reminded that there is no need to read the whole examination paper before beginning to select answers to the questions posed.

3. You must ensure that BEFORE the close of the examination all of your answers to the questions have been correctly entered on the answer sheet. If you leave a question unanswered for any reason, it will not receive a mark.

4. You may make any notes you wish on the question papers.

1. YATES, an adult male, has been arrested for the offence of murder and authorisation has been given for him to be held incommunicado. TI HAYES approaches DC TRUMP and asks him the maximum time that YATES can be held incommunicado if all the relevant authorities have been obtained.

   To comply under s. 5 or s. 6 or both of PACE 1984, rights may be delayed if the person is in police detention, as in PACE s. 118(2) for an indictable offence, and has not been charged. Which of the following is correct for DC TRUMP to tell TI HAYES?

   A 12 hours.
   B 24 hours.
   C 36 hours.
   D 48 hours.

2. CLAY knows that BANNER is having an affair and blackmails him, stating that if he does not give him some money and goods he will tell BANNER's wife of his affair. In response to the demand, BANNER gives CLAY £100 and a small gold necklace. CLAY keeps the money for himself and gives the necklace to his girlfriend, TRENT, as a gift. TRENT thinks this is suspicious but keeps the necklace. A few days later TRENT overhears CLAY bragging to his friends of his blackmail of BANNER and TRENT now knows that the necklace is stolen, but she likes it so much that she decides to keep it.

   Which of the following is correct with regards to any criminal responsibility of TRENT?

   A TRENT commits the offence of theft when she realises the necklace is stolen and decides to keep it.
   B TRENT commits the offence of handling stolen goods when she first accepts the necklace as a gift.
   C TRENT commits the offence of handling stolen goods when she overhears that the necklace is stolen and decides to keep it.
   D TRENT does not commit theft or commit handling stolen goods as goods obtained by blackmail are not property of the purpose of handling.

3. GRANT and MUSTOW have been living together for 12 months and MUSTOW is four months pregnant. One evening on returning home after a few beers they start a massive argument and GRANT realises from what MUSTOW says that the unborn child is not his and that her boss, HUDSON, is the father. Enraged by this, GRANT says *'I will kill that little bastard before it is born'*, intending that the threat would be feared by MUSTOW. MUSTOW, however, is not frightened by this as she knows when GRANT calms down he would never carry out the threat.

Considering the offence of making a threat to kill (contrary to s. 16 of the Offences Against the Person Act 1861), which of the following statements is correct?

A GRANT commits the offence as he had the intention that threat to kill would cause fear.

B GRANT does not commit the offence as the threat was made to a pregnant woman's unborn child before its birth.

C GRANT does not commit the offence as the threat to kill was to the future and not immediate.

D GRANT does not commit the offence as although he intended the threat to be feared, the threat was not actually feared by MUSTOW.

4. FRANKS has been aware for several months that he is HIV positive from an infected blood transfusion and it has taken him time to come to terms with his condition. This has resulted in him not having had sexual relations for some time. FRANKS goes away for a stag weekend to Blackpool with several other males. Later that night in a nightclub FRANKS befriends OSBOURNE and she invites him back to her hotel. At the hotel she goes to the bathroom and undresses, puts on a robe and on returning to the bedroom she removes a couple of bottles from the mini-bar. OSBOURNE suggests FRANKS makes himself more comfortable so he takes off all his clothes; they then have full protected sexual intercourse (penis to vagina using a condom). A few days later OSBOURNE is informed of FRANKS's condition and reports the offence of rape, stating that she would not have had sex with FRANKS had she known of his HIV.

Which of the following statements is correct in relation to FRANKS's liability?

A FRANKS commits rape in these circumstances as he has a duty to declare his sexually transmittable disease.

B FRANKS would be guilty if he had not taken measures to protect the victim by wearing a condom.

C FRANKS would not be guilty of rape as OSBOURNE had consented to the sexual intercourse.

D FRANKS would not commit rape but would be guilty of assault by penetration.

5. PC KITCHENER is out on patrol when he sees RYDER in the local park with what appears to be an electric stun gun. RYDER willingly hands over the electric stun gun for examination by PC KITCHENER. RYDER states that it is broken and does not work. PC KITCHENER examines the electric stun gun and then arrests RYDER for possession of a prohibited weapon in a public place.

Does RYDER commit an offence of possessing or distributing prohibited weapons or ammunition (contrary to s. 5 of the Firearms Act 1968)?

A Yes, RYDER commits the offence even if the stun gun is not working.
B No, an electrical stun gun is not a prohibited weapon under the Firearms Act 1968.
C Yes, RYDER would commit the offence if the electric stun gun was working.
D No, an electric stun gun is not a firearm, within the Firearms Act 1968.

6. HAINES arrives at a driving test centre for a practical driving test for a car. HAINES shows driving documents to the tester covering the photograph with his thumb; however, the documents shown to the tester are that of his cousin KEEN. HAINES intends to take the test for KEEN because KEEN has failed on his last two attempts. This ruse does not work and the police attend.

Relating to an offence of fraud contrary to s. 2 of the Fraud Act 2006 (fraud by false representation) which of the following statements is correct?

A Neither HAINES nor KEEN are guilty of the offence as a driving licence pass certificate is not property under the Fraud Act 2006.
B Both HAINES and KEEN are guilty of the offence; even though it was HAINES who made the false representation, it can be inferred that KEEN was complicit in the false representation.
C Because there was no pass certificate issued, both HAINES and KEEN would be guilty of attempting to commit the offence.
D Only HAINES is guilty of the offence as he was the person who made the false representation, it cannot be inferred that KEEN was complicit.

7. The Halton Shopping Centre is being targeted by a small gang of shoplifters during the Christmas rush and you wish to use the CCTV at the shopping centre for non-urgent directed surveillance, to gather intelligence and identify the offenders. This is both proportionate and necessary.

Which of the following is correct with regard to persons who can authorise directed surveillance under the Regulation of Investigatory Powers Act (RIPA) 2000?

A It must be authorised in writing by an ACC/Commander or above and will last for a period of one month.
B It must be authorised in writing by an ACC/Commander or above and will last for a period of three months.
C It must be authorised in writing by a superintendent or above and will last for a period of one month.
D It must be authorised in writing by a superintendent or above and will last for a period of three months.

8. PINE is an 18-year-old male student at the local college and does not have much money and his mobile phone does not have a camera. JAMES is a 16-year-old female friend of PINE's and she has agreed to allow PINE to take naked pictures of her just for fun. PINE, in order to take the photographs of JAMES, goes to the local camera shop and manages to steal a camera.

Considering s. 62 of the Sexual Offences Act 2003 (committing a criminal offence with intent to commit a sexual offence), which of the statements below is correct?

A PINE does not commit the offence because taking indecent photographs is not a relevant offence under this section.

B PINE commits the offence in these circumstances.

C PINE does not commit the offence because JAMES is 16 years or over.

D PINE would commit the offence under this section only if he took the indecent photographs.

9. HANCOCK is wanted for a serious armed robbery where he used a revolver to threaten staff. He resides in a small block of flats and a team of armed officers go to his flat in the early hours of the morning to arrest him. The officers surround the premises but, before they go up the stairs to his flat, HANCOCK appears at the top landing and fires two shots at PC FLINT, one of the armed officers. FLINT returns fire but a split second before he does HANCOCK pulls his girlfriend, SIMPSON, in front of him as a shield. The officers return fire and kill SIMPSON. HANCOCK then places his hands in the air in surrender and is formally arrested.

Which of the following statements is correct with regards to the criminal liability of HANCOCK?

A HANCOCK is guilty of the murder of SIMPSON.

B HANCOCK is guilty of voluntary manslaughter of SIMPSON.

C HANCOCK is guilty of involuntary manslaughter by unlawful act.

D HANCOCK is not liable in these circumstances for the death of SIMPSON.

10. SHEFFIELD is attacked and robbed by TAYLOR (who is a stranger to SHEFFIELD). DC McCUBBIN is first to arrive at the scene of the offence and quickly obtains a first description of TAYLOR from SHEFFIELD. DC McCUBBIN places SHEFFIELD in an unmarked police vehicle and drives SHEFFIELD around the local area to see if he can identify the person responsible for the offence. They drive along a busy street with a cafe on one side of the road and a pub on the other. People are outside both premises and SHEFFIELD is looking intently at a group outside the cafe. DC McCUBBIN sees a person who matches the description given by SHEFFIELD standing outside the pub with a group of people and asks SHEFFIELD to look closely at the group outside the pub. As a result, SHEFFIELD identifies TAYLOR who is in the group outside the pub and is subsequently arrested by other officers searching the area.

In relation to Code D of the Codes of Practice, which of the following comments is correct?

A Code D has not been complied with as once a first description of an offender has been obtained from an eye-witness they should not take part in any 'street' identification process.

B Code D has not been complied with as DC McCUBBIN is not allowed to draw the attention of SHEFFIELD to a particular group.

C Code D has not been complied with as at least two officers must be present when such a 'street' identification process takes place.

D Code D of the Codes of Practice has been complied with by the officer.

11. INGRAM and COLLIER are chatting outside INGRAM's house, discussing a three-month cruise around the world that INGRAM returned from yesterday. PC TUCKER arrives at INGRAM's house and speaks to INGRAM to establish his identity. Once the officer has established INGRAM's identity, he takes hold of him and arrests him for an offence of burglary that occurred one month ago at a shop in Bradford (a lawful arrest). INGRAM knows he is innocent as he was out of the country (in the Caribbean at that time) when the offence was committed and, intending to resist his own arrest, he kicks the officer in the leg. Believing INGRAM to be innocent, COLLIER mistakenly believes that the officer is acting unlawfully and, intending to help INGRAM resist arrest, COLLIER punches the officer in the face.

Considering only the offence of assault with intent to resist arrest (contrary to s. 38 of the Offences Against the Person Act 1861), which of the following comments is true?

A Both men would have a defence to the offence in these circumstances.

B Neither INGRAM's genuine belief in his own innocence nor COLLIER's mistaken belief that the officer was acting unlawfully will provide either of them with a defence.

C INGRAM's genuine belief in his own innocence would provide him with a defence; COLLIER's mistaken belief that the officer was acting unlawfully will not.

D INGRAM's genuine belief in his own innocence would not provide him with a defence; COLLIER does not need a defence as he has not committed the offence as it is only committed when resisting your own arrest.

12. WILSON has been arrested for drug-related crimes. At the custody block the arresting officer informs the custody sergeant that there is evidence that WILSON has swallowed some drugs. WILSON's detention is authorised and the officers wish to carry out an X-ray or ultrasound scan on WILSON.

In order to comply with s. 55A of PACE 1984 which of the following statements is correct?

A The drug swallowed must be a Class A drug and have been for supply or export. The authority required is that of an inspector (along with the consent of WILSON) and no force can be used.

B The drug swallowed must be a Class A and have been for supply or export. The authority required is that of an inspector and force can be used.

C The drug swallowed can be a Class A, B or C and have been for supply or export. The authority required is that of an inspector (along with the consent of WILSON) and no force can be used.

D The drug swallowed can be a Class A, B or C and have been for supply or export. The authority required is that of an inspector and force can be used.

13. BARCLAY, an adult male, meets FORD, an adult female, in a bar and after a couple of drinks they go back to his flat. After a drink and some kissing, BARCLAY becomes aggressive towards FORD and proceeds to commit sexual acts with FORD without consent. He first forces her to the ground and inserts a rubber dildo into her mouth, then BARCLAY inserts his fingers in her anus followed by the rubber dildo into her vagina, and he then encourages his dog to insert its penis into her vagina.

Considering the offences of assault by penetration (contrary to s. 2 of the Sexual Offences Act 2003) only, which of the following statements is correct as to BARCLAY's liability?

A BARCLAY does not commit this particular sexual offence.

B BARCLAY commits this offence when he inserts the dildo into her mouth, his fingers in her anus and the dildo in her vagina.

C BARCLAY commits this offence only when he inserts his fingers in her anus and the dildo in her vagina.

D BARCLAY commits this offence when he inserts his fingers in her anus and the dildo in her vagina and when he encourages his dog to insert its penis in her vagina.

14. ATKINS is director of Guy Wilkes Ltd, a manufacturing company. Wilkes Ltd owns 20 acres of land a short distance from the factory which over the years has been used for testing off-road vehicles. The land is no longer of use to the company, but has a value for agricultural purposes of about £5,000 per acre. ATKINS is tasked by the company to sell the land on behalf of the company with a view to the company making a profit from the sale of the land. ATKINS sells the land to himself at £1,000 per acre thinking that once he owns the land he can sell it for the correct market value and make a large amount of money.

Considering the legislation with regard to an offence of theft (under s. 1 of the Theft Act 1968) and specifically the law under s. 4(2) of the Theft Act 1968, does ATKINS commit theft?

A Yes, if you could prove that he had rented the land first.
B No, as land can never be classed as property for the purposes of theft.
C Yes, he commits the offence in these circumstances.
D No, because you can only steal items severed from the land.

15. Julie MULLEN is a single-parent mother and has a son, James MULLEN, aged 16; his girlfriend is Diane KINSELLA, aged 15. Julie is aware that James and Diane are having sex, albeit she does not allow them to have sex in her house. In view of this James and Diane visit his father, Adrian MULLEN, at weekends and he allows them to share a bedroom knowing that they have sex. Julie, her son James and Diane are going on holiday to Spain and when Julie books the holiday, James and Diane persuade Julie to allow them to share a bedroom. Julie does so knowing that they will have sex whilst on holiday in Spain.

In relation to s. 14 of the Sexual Offences Act 2003 (arranging or facilitating the commission of child sex offences), do either Julie or Adrian commit an offence?

A Adrian is guilty of facilitating and Julie is guilty of arranging sex for another (James).
B Neither is guilty of this offence as the arranging or facilitating sex for themselves or others is for persons aged 18 or over committing child offences.
C Adrian is guilty of the offence of facilitating but Julie is not guilty of arranging because the sex will not take place in this country.
D Adrian is guilty of the offence of facilitating because the sex has taken place; however, Julie will not be guilty until they take the holiday.

16. JAGGARD and BLOUNT have lived together for many years. JAGGARD is the dominant party in the relationship and has been aggressive and sexually abusive towards BLOUNT on several occasions, so much so that BLOUNT leaves JAGGARD. The two meet up at a restaurant to try and resolve their differences and are getting on very well. They go back to a hotel and become passionate with each other. JAGGARD asks BLOUNT to have sexual intercourse with him and BLOUNT agrees but on the strict understanding that JAGGARD will not ejaculate inside her. JAGGARD tells BLOUNT he will not and states he will withdraw his penis before ejaculation. As a result, the two have sexual intercourse. During intercourse, JAGGARD deliberately, against BLOUNT's wishes, ejaculates inside her.

Considering the law in relation to rape and consent under the Sexual Offences Act 2003 and the presumptions under ss. 75 and 76 of the Act, which of the following comments is correct?

A This is not an offence of rape as BLOUNT agreed to have sexual intercourse with JAGGARD.

B This is an offence of rape by JAGGARD as he has deprived BLOUNT of freedom of choice by ejaculating inside her (a crucial feature on which her original consent was based).

C This is an offence of rape; the presumption under s. 75 will apply.

D This is an offence of rape; the presumption under s. 76 will apply.

17. MINCHER and DUDLEY are old friends who used to be at university together. They meet in a pub for a reunion drink—MINCHER drinks a couple of pints of lager but DUDLEY is driving so she is only drinking lemonade. During their conversation, MINCHER reminds DUDLEY of the fun they used to have when they took drugs together and states that he has some LSD with him and asks DUDLEY if she would like some for 'old times' sake'. DUDLEY politely refuses. DUDLEY visits the toilet of the pub and while she is away, MINCHER places a 'tab' of LSD in her lemonade. He swallows some LSD himself and when DUDLEY returns from the toilet she drinks her lemonade, swallowing the LSD in the process. The drug intoxicates MINCHER and DUDLEY who both begin to behave in an extremely erratic fashion resulting in GALLON (the landlord of the pub) requiring the two to leave the premises. MINCHER and DUDLEY attack GALLON causing him actual bodily harm (s. 47 of the Offences Against the Person Act 1861). The police are called and MINCHER and DUDLEY are arrested.

In relation to the law regarding intoxication and its use as a 'general defence', which of the following comments is correct?

A Intoxication is only relevant when the source of the intoxication is alcohol.

B As a s. 47 assault is a 'basic' intent offence, intoxication (whether it be from drink or drugs) would have no relevance for either of the accused.

C As DUDLEY was involuntarily intoxicated, she would be able to raise 'intoxication' in defence to a charge of s. 47 assault.

D It does not matter that MINCHER was voluntarily intoxicated as a result of taking the LSD—he could still raise the issue of intoxication in defence to a charge of s. 47 assault.

18. MASON and BAYTON work in the same office building and sometimes have dealings with each other in a professional capacity. As far as MASON is concerned, the two are work colleagues and nothing more. However, BAYTON thinks that MASON is in love with her and is obsessed with MASON as a result. BAYTON publishes a statement on her Facebook page telling all of her friends that she has received a letter from MASON telling her that he is in love with and wants to marry her (this is a total fabrication by BAYTON). This causes MASON some embarrassment in his workplace but nothing more as he laughs it off as a joke. The following day, BAYTON sends an email to MASON telling him that she loves him and that if she sees him with another woman she will kill herself. As a result of BAYTON's continued behaviour, MASON's performance at work deteriorates due to stress brought on by BAYTON's activities.

Which of the following comments is correct in respect of the law regarding the offence of stalking (under s. 4A of the Protection from Harassment Act 1997)?

A The offence under s. 4A has been committed by BAYTON when she publishes the statement about the love letter on her Facebook page.

B The offence under s. 4A has been committed by BAYTON when she sends the email to MASON threatening to kill herself if she sees him with another woman and because of the consequent effect it has on MASON.

C The offence under s. 4A has not been committed by BAYTON as she has not caused MASON to fear, on two occasions, that violence will be used against him.

D The offence under s. 4A has not been committed because the course of conduct pursued by BAYTON does not amount to 'stalking'.

19. PCs HALL and SIMON are directed to a report of a high-value robbery at a jewellers. On arrival, the officers speak to the owner of the shop who provides them with the description of two men who have made off with at least £2 million pounds' worth of jewellery. The officers carry out an immediate search of the area and find, arrest and caution one of the men responsible, GOULD. GOULD is searched but does not have any of the stolen jewellery on his person. PC HALL asks GOULD *'Where is the jewellery?'* to which GOULD does not respond. PC SIMON asks GOULD *'C'mon, this isn't a couple of gold rings, this is two million quids' worth, we need to know now, where is it?'* GOULD replies, *'My mate has it, we split up after the robbery and we're supposed to meet up later on tonight at his house, the jewels will be there in about 30 minutes' time.'* GOULD then tells the officers the address of his associate.

Which of the following comments is true in relation to the behaviour of the officers?

A The interview is illegal as Code C of the PACE Codes of Practice states that any interview of a person under arrest must take place at a police station.

B The officers should not have interviewed GOULD without the authorisation of an officer of at least the rank of superintendent.

C The interview of a person under arrest should take place at a police station unless waiting to do so would lead to physical harm to people; therefore the interview of GOULD in the vehicle is not permitted in this situation.

D The officers are acting correctly if they think any delay in interviewing GOULD could hinder the recovery of property obtained in consequence of the commission of the robbery offence.

20. PC SLATER is on patrol and is dispatched to a small wooded area where a person has reported finding an insecure shed. On arrival, PC SLATER cannot find the person who called the police but identifies the shed. On entering the shed, the officer finds several guns and rifles and other paraphernalia for supporting a terrorist group. PC SLATER immediately tapes off the area under his power to designate under s. 34 of the Terrorism Act 2000 (by reason of urgency) for an investigation.

Which of the following statements is correct with regard to further compliance under s. 34 and s. 35 of the Terrorism Act 2000?

A An officer of at least the rank of superintendent is informed and if continued designation is confirmed the initial designation can be only for a maximum of 7 days.

B An officer of at least the rank of superintendent is informed and if continued designation is confirmed the initial designation can be only for a maximum of 14 days.

C An officer of at least the rank of ACC/Commander is informed and if continued designation is confirmed the initial designation can be only for a maximum of 7 days.

D An officer of at least the rank of ACC/Commander is informed and if continued designation is confirmed the initial designation can be only for a maximum of 14 days.

21. JEFFERSON is driving around late at night and sees a rubber dingy on the driveway of a house. JEFFERSON decides to take the rubber dingy as his friend HINES could use it at weekends on his fishing trips. JEFFERSON places the dingy on the roof rack of his car and drives off. JEFFERSON is later stopped by police and arrested.

Considering the offence of taking a conveyance without the owner's consent, contrary to s. 12(1) of the Theft Act 1968, which of the following statements is correct?

A JEFFERSON has committed the offence in these circumstances.

B JEFFERSON has attempted the offence.

C JEFFERSON has not committed the offence as the rubber dingy is not a mechanically propelled vehicle.

D JEFFERSON has not committed the offence as he is not the person who is going to use the dingy.

22. DOBBS is a well-known drug dealer and also owns a night club. He is notorious in the area for his criminal behaviour, but all prosecutions have been unsuccessful. DOBBS asks READ, a local builder, to quote him for a new roof to his garage block. READ's quote is for £4,500—a realistic price for the work—and DOBBS tells READ that he will pay in cash. READ suspects that the money is from DOBBS's drug-dealing activities, but accepts the job as his business is struggling. READ completes the work and is paid in cash and declares the full amount of this as income on his accounts. DOBBS is arrested 18 months later and a successful prosecution brought against him for drug dealing.

Does READ commit an offence contrary to s. 329 of the Proceeds of Crime Act 2002 (acquisition, use and possession of criminal property)?

A No offence is committed as DOBBS was arrested more than 12 months after the money was paid to READ.

B Yes, READ is guilty of the offence as he suspected that the money came from criminal activity.

C No, as READ received the money as adequate consideration for the work he completed.

D Yes, because he accepted cash suspecting DOBBS's criminal activities and this assisted in its disposal.

23. Officers raid 76 The Banks, Salford following intelligence of the persons responsible for several burglaries in the area residing at the address. The suspects are arrested and taken into custody. PC HALDER is placed at the gate of the front of the property because of local media interest, just inside a taped off cordon, whilst other officers search the property. After a short while a news team with cameras set up opposite the premises outside the taped off area. STONE, a brother of one of those arrested, arrives at the property and is very annoyed that his brother has been arrested. STONE approaches PC HALDER and leaning over the tape he shouts, 'You fucking pig, if these cameras weren't here, you shit, I'd beat the crap out of you!'

Which of the following statements is correct with regard to offences of assault only?

A STONE commits the offence of s. 39 common assault as he intended PC HALDER to apprehend the immediate infliction of unlawful force.

B STONE only commits the offence of attempt s. 39 common assault as there was no battery.

C STONE commits the offence of assaulting a constable in the execution of his duty even though he used only words.

D STONE does not commit an assault in these circumstances.

24. Henry SINCLAIR is an 18-year-old male and lives with his step-sister, Jayne RAYNOR, who is 16 years old and both their respective parents, his father and her mother; both the parents are widowed. Henry and Jayne have been step-brother and sister for the last five years. During this time they have become very close and have fallen in love; however, because of their very religious upbringing they have remained totally celibate. Henry asks Jayne to marry him and her mother gives the appropriate legal consent. They marry two weeks before Jayne's 17th birthday.

Considering offences contrary to s. 25 of the Sexual Offences Act 2003 (Sexual Activity with Child Family Members), which of the following statements is correct?

A Henry and Jayne cannot have sex until she is 17.
B Henry and Jayne can have sex because they are married.
C Henry and Jayne cannot have sex until she is 18.
D Henry and Jayne can have sex as they are not blood relatives and she is 16 years or over.

25. SPEED is being interviewed for an offence of burglary and has answered 'no comment' to the questions asked of him. He realises that the police have a lot of evidence against him and so asks for a short break while he gathers his thoughts. As it will be a short break, no persons leave the interview room.

To comply with Code E of PACE, which of the following statements is correct with regard to procedures to be taken for short breaks in interviews?

A If a short break is taken then it should be treated as the end of an interview; the relevant sealing and signatures are required.
B If a short break is taken then both the interviewer and the suspect can remain in the interview room and the recording media may be stopped; when the interview recommences the same recording media can be used.
C If a short break is taken then both the interviewer and the suspect can remain in the interview room and the recording media must not be stopped and must remain on for the duration of the short break.
D As this is a short break then the officers must leave the room to allow the detainee to gather their thoughts but the recording media can be switched off and when the interview recommences the same recording material can be used.

26. BUCHANAN is a British citizen who owns several holiday homes in Italy. He is visiting Naples when he sees ALI, a refugee from Libya, begging on a street. BUCHANAN approaches ALI and asks her if she is interested in working for him as a maid in one of his holiday homes a short distance away on the Amalfi Coast of Italy and tells her the job comes with food and lodging. ALI is delighted at the prospect and replies that she is interested. BUCHANAN tells her that she will need to meet him in a side street around the corner from their current location in one hour and he will drive her to the holiday home. BUCHANAN actually intends to take ALI to the house to exploit her by forcing her into prostitution. One hour later, BUCHANAN meets ALI and drives her to the holiday home. During the journey, ALI becomes suspicious of BUCHANAN and manages to escape when he stops for fuel.

Which of the following statements is correct in relation to BUCHANAN's liability for the offence of human trafficking (contrary to s. 2 of the Modern Slavery Act 2015)?

A As the activity (arranging ALI's travel) takes place in Naples this would not constitute an offence under s. 2 of the Act.

B The offence has been committed by BUCHANAN but only when he actually picks ALI up and drives her to his holiday home with a view to exploiting her.

C The offence has been committed by BUCHANAN as soon as he arranged the travel of ALI with a view to her being exploited.

D The offence has not been committed as BUCHANAN intended to exploit ALI outside the United Kingdom (he intended to exploit her in Naples).

27. TENANT, an adult male, is working in York for the week as a representative of a chemical company. In the bar of the hotel he engages in conversation with HANNAH, an adult female. TENANT buys HANNAH several drinks and they start becoming very tactile with each other. Unbeknown to TENANT, HANNAH is a paranoid schizophrenic (a mental condition) so when TENANT suggests they go to his room for sex HANNAH agrees solely because of her condition, believing that it is right to do so. In TENANT's bedroom they have oral sex.

Does TENANT commit an offence of sexual activity with a mentally disordered person contrary to s. 30 of the Sexual Offences Act 2003?

A No, TENANT has to be aware that HANNAH was suffering from a mental disorder.

B Yes, the offence includes oral sex and there does not have to be full intercourse.

C No, as TENANT has to have sexual intercourse with HANNAH for the offence to be complete.

D Yes, but as TENANT was not aware of HANNAH's mental disorder it is therefore a summary only offence.

28. FORD's friend, MORRIS, is allowing FORD to stay at his house whilst he is on holiday. FORD has full use of the house but he is there to look after MORRIS's dog. FORD is a drug addict and he receives a phone call from his drug dealer saying that he wants the £100 he owes him. FORD, not having the cash to hand but hoping to have it before MORRIS returns, takes MORRIS's computer to the pawn shop and raises the £100 needed to pay off his drug dealer which he then does. Unfortunately, FORD does not manage to find the money needed to recover the computer.

Considering the offence of theft (under s. 1 of the Theft Act 1968) and the law relating to s. 6 of the Theft Act 1968 (intention to permanently deprive), is FORD liable for theft?

A No, FORD is not liable because he had legal access to the property from MORRIS.
B Yes, FORD is liable if you can prove that he would never have the resources to recover the computer from the pawn shop.
C No, FORD is not liable because he had no intention to permanently deprive when he exchanged the computer for cash.
D Yes, FORD is liable as it amounts to treating the property as his own.

29. MAY is short of money and wants to go to his friend's for a couple of days. MAY's friend lives in York so MAY goes to the local transport cafe—where haulage lorries park up while their drivers have refreshments—and sneaks into the rear of one of the lorries destined to deliver goods to York. When the lorry stops on the outskirts of York, MAY gets out of the lorry and walks towards his friend's house. Whilst walking through a 'red light' area he is approached by LOMAS a street prostitute who offers to masturbate him for £10. Being too good an opportunity to miss, and having no intention of paying LOMAS, he allows LOMAS to masturbate him. Once LOMAS has finished, he runs off and later arrives at his friend's house.

Which of the following statements is correct with regards to the criminal responsibility of MAY under s.11 of the Fraud Act 2006 (obtaining services dishonestly)?

A MAY commits two offences: when he gets a free ride to York and in non-payment to the prostitute.
B MAY only commits the offence when he does not pay the prostitute.
C MAY only commits the offence when he gets a free ride to York.
D MAY does not commit any offence in these circumstances as neither the free ride nor the masturbation by the prostitute are classed as a service.

30. PARSON (aged 19 years) shares a two-bedroom flat with CLARK (aged 17 years). PARSON pays 70% of the rent and other expenses because he earns more than CLARK; they are just flatmates. PARSON, however, believes this to be unjust and persuades CLARK that he needs some form of reward for paying the majority of the bills. PARSON persuades CLARK to masturbate him once a week as compensation; CLARK does not want to do this but complies. The owner of the flat puts up the rent and PARSON now decides that CLARK need not masturbate him anymore but will have to prostitute herself as she cannot pay any more towards the bills; she has no option but to agree to PARSON's requests. A couple of times a week CLARK performs sexual acts with other men for money.

Considering s. 4 of the Sexual Offences Act 2003 (causing a person to engage in sexual activity without consent), which of the statements below is correct?

A PARSON only commits this offence when he forces CLARK to masturbate him.
B PARSON does not commit any offences under s. 4 because CLARK is over the age of 16.
C PARSON commits this offence when he forces her to masturbate him and when he forces her to prostitute herself.
D PARSON only commits this offence when he forces her to prostitute herself.

31. Section 1 of the Child Abduction Act 1984 provides a defence whereby a person does not commit an offence under this section by taking or sending the child out of the United Kingdom without the appropriate consent if either he has a child arrangement order in force in respect of the child or he is a special guardian of the child. This defence under s. 1 of not requiring the appropriate consent has time limits for the sending or taking of the child out of the United Kingdom.

In relation to those time limits, which of the statements below is correct?

A Both persons with a child arrangement order and special guardians can take or send the child out of the United Kingdom without the appropriate consent for a period of less than one month.
B Persons with a child arrangement order can take or send the child out of the United Kingdom without the appropriate consent for less than one month and special guardians for less than three months.
C Both persons with a child arrangement order and special guardians can take or send the child out of the United Kingdom without the appropriate consent for a period of less than three months.
D Persons with a child arrangement order can take or send the child out of the United Kingdom without the appropriate consent for less than three months and special guardians for less than one month.

32. HATTON has been arrested for a motoring offence; his detention has been authorised and he has been placed in a cell while the officers make further enquiries. HATTON is disgusted by his arrest and therefore to cause trouble and reckless as to the consequences, he places the blanket provided down the toilet in the cell. HATTON then continually flushes the toilet. When the custody sergeant makes his first check on HATTON, the concrete floor of the cell is flooded and the blanket is soaking wet.

Considering the offence of criminal damage (contrary to s. 1(1) of the Criminal Damage Act 1971), does HATTON commit the offence?

A No, HATTON would not commit criminal damage in these circumstances as both the floor and the blanket could be dried out without any resulting damage to either.

B Yes, HATTON would commit criminal damage to the blanket, but not the floor as it could be dried out undamaged.

C No, HATTON would not commit criminal damage in these circumstances as there was no intention to damage property; it was just frustration at his circumstances.

D Yes, HATTON would be guilty of criminal damage to both the blanket and the floor.

33. FRANKLIN is arrested in Glasgow for an offence of minor theft and is dealt with. Officers dealing with the enquiry ascertain that FRANKLIN is circulated as wanted by officers at Plymouth Police Station, in the Devon and Cornwall police area, for an offence of rape. Officers travel from Plymouth to Glasgow by car and arrive at 13:00 hours. They do not question FRANKLIN and start their return journey at 13:30. They cross the border into England at 15:30 hours and continue their journey. At 18:00 hours, they stop at Stafford Police Station to use the toilet and canteen facilities. They then continue their journey and at 21:00 hours they stop at Exeter Police Station, a police station in the force area of Devon and Cornwall Police to use the toilet and the canteen facilities. Continuing their journey, they arrive at Plymouth Police Station at 22:00 hours.

With regards to the offence of rape in Plymouth, when does the relevant time commence?

A When they stop at Exeter Police Station at 21:00 hours in the force area where FRANKLIN is wanted.

B When they arrive at Plymouth Police Station at 22:00 hours at the police station where FRANKLIN is wanted.

C When they cross the border into England and Wales area at 15:30 hours.

D When they stop at Stafford Police Station at 18:00 hours, the first police station in England and Wales area.

34. DC FAYED is working in the Criminal Investigation Department at his station when he receives good-quality intelligence from a trusted source in relation to the location of a large amount of stolen goods. The stolen property is alleged to be located at five different premises and after briefly discussing the matter with his supervisor, DC FAYED decides to make an application to search all the premises (an 'all premises' warrant). Due to the nature of the intelligence received by DC FAYED, he decides to request that the warrant allow entry to the target premises on multiple occasions.

In relation to the procedures under ss. 15 and 16 of the Police and Criminal Evidence Act 1984 (application for a warrant and execution of a warrant) and Code B of the Codes of Practice, which of the following comments is correct?

A Applications for multiple premises and multiple entry warrants must be made with the written authority of an officer of at least the rank of superintendent (although in urgent cases where a superintendent is not readily available, the most senior officer on duty may authorise the application).

B Entry and search under such a warrant must be made within one month from the date of its issue.

C No premises may be entered or searched for the second or any subsequent time under a warrant which authorises multiple entries unless a police officer of at least the rank of inspector has, in writing, authorised that entry to those premises.

D If the warrant is an all premises warrant, no premises which are not specified in it may be entered and searched unless a police officer of at least the rank of superintendent has, in writing, authorised them to be entered.

35. WASHINGTON and DRISCOLL have an argument in a pub resulting in WASHINGTON threatening to give DRISCOLL a *'good old-fashioned black eye!'* DRISCOLL is frightened by WASHINGTON's threats and runs out of the pub and gets into his car to get away from the pub as fast as he can. He is inside his car when he sees WASHINGTON run out of the pub and towards him. DRISCOLL feels that he is going to be assaulted by WASHINGTON and so starts his car and drives towards WASHINGTON, hitting him and throwing him over the bonnet of the car and causing WASHINGTON serious physical injury. DRISCOLL is later charged with an offence of s. 20 grievous bodily harm against WASHINGTON.

Considering the general defence of duress of circumstances, which of the following comments is correct?

A DRISCOLL could not advance the defence as he was not in the situation where the threat to him was one of death or serious injury.

B DRISCOLL would be able to use the defence as the offence that he is accused of committing is one that involves serious injury.

C The defence is available in answer to a variety of different charges but not to one of s. 20 grievous bodily harm.

D The defence is available to DRISCOLL as he is charged with an offence involving causing injury to another—if it were a property-related charge then the defence would be unavailable.

36. Section 18(2) of the Modern Slavery Act 2015 allows a slavery and trafficking prevention order (STPO) to be made to prevent a person travelling to any specified country outside the United Kingdom, any country other than a country specified in the order or any country outside the United Kingdom.

What is the maximum time that a prohibition order can be fixed initially and made by the court?

A Four years.
B Five years.
C Six years.
D Seven years.

37. BORG is arrested for being a member of a proscribed organisation (an offence under s. 11 of the Terrorism Act 2000). The investigation that follows reveals that BORG rents a storage facility near to his home address and this is subsequently searched. Inside the storage facility is a box which is found to contain several electronic timers which could be used in the manufacture of explosive devices.

Considering only the offence of making or possessing an explosive substance under suspicious circumstances (contrary to s. 4 of the Explosive Substances Act 1883), which of the following statements is correct?

A The offence has been committed by BORG as he has the electronic timers under his control.
B BORG has not committed the offence as an electronic timer is not classed as an 'explosive substance'.
C The offence has been committed by BORG but the consent of the Director of Public Prosecutions would be required before a prosecution can be brought.
D The offence has not been committed as BORG does not have the electronic timers in his possession.

38. UNWIN and GAYNOR are at UNWIN's house watching a film. From the conversation GAYNOR realises that UNWIN has been having sex with her boyfriend and confronts her. UNWIN admits that they are having sex. Enraged, GAYNOR picks up a pair of scissors on the coffee table and stabs UNWIN in the chest (a s. 18 wounding contrary to the Offences Against the Person Act 1861) and GAYNOR leaves the house. GAYNOR's description is circulated and a passing patrol sees her on the street and arrests her for the s. 18 wounding. In GAYNOR's pocket they find an imitation firearm (a small pistol). The arresting officer PC DENTON comes to the CID office and asks if GAYNOR has committed any firearm offences.

Considering s. 17(2) of the Firearms Act 1968 (possessing a firearm while committing a sch. 1 offence), which of the following is correct with regard to the liability of GAYNOR?

A For the offence to be committed it must be a real firearm.
B Mere possession at the time of arrest for a sch. 1 offence is sufficient.
C Section 18 wounding is not included in sch. 1.
D You would need to prove that she also had the firearm with her at the time of the s. 18 wounding even though it was not used.

39. SUTTER is walking home one night because he has missed the last bus. SUTTER is frustrated by this and walks up the road looking for cars he could steal for his journey home. SUTTER approaches a Vauxhall Astra and he can see the car keys on the driver's seat but the vehicle is locked. SUTTER smashes the driver's window, gets into the car and starts the engine and drives off. It is a frosty evening and when he slowly takes a small right-hand bend the vehicle slides on the ice and smashes into the front garden wall of a house. Police attend the scene and arrest SUTTER.

Considering an offence of aggravated vehicle-taking (contrary to s. 12A of the Theft Act 1968), which of the following statements is correct?

A SUTTER does not commit this offence.
B SUTTER commits this offence when he damages the vehicle for the original taking but not the damage caused to the vehicle in the accident because there must be evidence of careless driving.
C SUTTER commits this offence when he damages the vehicle for the original taking and the damage caused to vehicle during the accident as you do not have to prove careless driving.
D SUTTER does not commit this offence when he damages the vehicle for the original taking but does with regards to the damage caused to the vehicle during the accident.

40. WENTWORTH is a 17-year-old male who has been going out with SMYTH, a 15-year-old female, for three months and they have not had sex yet. One evening, whilst babysitting for SMYTH's older sister, they are alone. WENTWORTH, who knows that SMYTH does not want to risk having full sex as she is concerned about becoming pregnant, suggests that he uses a dildo on her. WENTWORTH knows SMYTH has a small dildo in her handbag. SMYTH is excited by the thought of WENTWORTH using the dildo on her and she agrees. WENTWORTH then uses the dildo on SMYTH.

What would be the appropriate charge for WENTWORTH in these circumstances?

A WENTWORTH commits an offence contrary to s. 3 of the Sexual Offences Act 2003.
B WENTWORTH commits an offence contrary to s. 13 of the Sexual Offences Act 2003.
C WENTWORTH commits an offence contrary to s. 9 of the Sexual Offences Act 2003.
D Both WENTWORTH and SMYTH commit an offence contrary to s. 9 of the Sexual Offences Act 2003 as they are both under the age of 18.

41. LUMLEY, an adult male, is questioned by DC ATHERLEY with regard to two offences of burglary and he admits his part in the crimes. At court, he is sentenced to a hospital order owing to his drug habits and mental state. After four months he is released from hospital.

There is no case to appeal, so in relation to the retention periods of relevant case material, how long does DC ATHERLEY need to retain the material?

   A Once LUMLEY is released, the case material can be disposed of as he served more than three months of a hospital order.
   B Once LUMLEY is released, the case material can be disposed of as there is no need to retain it when a hospital order has been given.
   C The material must be kept for at least 12 months after his release, if his sentence had been custodial; however, for hospital orders it only needs to be retained for six months from the date of release.
   D The material must be retained for a period of at least six months from the date of the hospital order.

42. FROST, aged 14 years, has been the victim of a sexual assault, whereby she was dragged into some bushes in the local park and digitally penetrated by the offender whilst he masturbated. The offender was wearing a balaclava so there is no possibility of using facial identification procedures. The scene has not been identified as the victim cannot be sure where the attack took place and from the medical examination of FROST, although there is evidence of such abuse, no DNA of the offender has been found. However, the victim's statement states that the offender had shaved off his pubic hair and had a small cut above his penis. PACEY has been arrested in connection with this offence and DC TRANTER, the officer in the case, wants to take a photograph of PACEY's genital region to prove or disprove his involvement in the offence, also knowing full well that PACEY's pubic hair will have grown by the time the matter gets to court. PACEY will not consent to the photograph being taken.

To comply with s. 54A(1) of PACE 1984, which of the following statements is correct?

   A Authority can be given by a superintendent or above for a photograph to be taken and if the suspect still refuses reasonable force can be used to take it.
   B Authority can be given by a superintendent or above for a photograph to be taken and if the suspect still refuses a warning will be given that the court can draw an inference from his refusal.
   C Authority can be given by an officer of at least inspector rank or above for a photograph to be taken and if the suspect still refuses reasonable force can be used to take it.
   D Authority can be given by an officer of at least inspector rank or above for a photograph to be taken, and if the suspect still refuses a warning will be given that the court can draw an inference from his refusal.

43. DC FAIRBAIRN is dealing with HAKIN who has been arrested for an offence of fraud. HAKIN has requested the services of his solicitor, TAYLOR, who arrives at the station and is taken into a consultation room where disclosure takes place. After TAYLOR has a consultation with HAKIN, an interview takes place. At the beginning of the interview DC FAIRBAIRN cautions HAKIN and asks if he understands the caution. At this point TAYLOR states that he has explained the meaning of the caution to his client and that his client fully understands the caution.

What course of action should DC FAIRBAIRN take?

A If it appears to DC FAIRBAIRN that HAKIN does not understand the caution, he should go on to explain it in his own words.

B The fact that HAKIN has been told the meaning of the caution by his solicitor means that DC FAIRBAIRN need not go on to explain it.

C As long as the caution has been given, then DC FAIRBAIRN may continue the interview without any further explanation of it.

D Providing a record is made of the fact that the solicitor has explained the meaning of the caution to HAKIN, DC FAIRBAIRN need not go on to explain it.

44. BUTLER, a 23-year-old male, has attended the police station voluntarily to answer questions under caution. He is one of a number of staff being interviewed in respect of theft by employees at the DIY warehouse. At the end of the audio interview, although he has been cooperative in the interview, BUTLER refuses to sign the seal.

Which of the statements below is the correct procedure in these circumstances?

A The senior officer (by rank or length of service) in the interview room will sign the seal as BUTLER is not in police detention and has attended voluntarily.

B An officer of at least the rank of inspector or if not available the custody officer or, if the suspect has not been arrested a sergeant shall be called into the interview room and asked to sign the seal.

C An officer of at least the rank of inspector or if not available the custody officer must sign the seal.

D An officer of at least the rank of inspector must sign the seal.

45. JAKEMAN, an adult male, has been arrested for an offence of burglary (a recordable offence) and is in police detention having been taken to the custody block of a designated police station. At the scene of the burglary there is a footprint made by trainer-style footwear. JAKEMAN has trainer-style footwear on when documented by the custody officer and you wish to take impressions of his trainers but JAKEMAN has refused.

Under s. 61A of PACE 1984 footwear impressions can be taken, but which of the statements below is correct?

A Authority is required from an officer of the rank of inspector or above and force can be used.

B Authority is required from an officer of the rank of inspector or above and force cannot be used but a warning can be given that a court can draw an inference from a refusal.

C Authority can be given by the custody sergeant and force can be used.

D A police officer can take an impression of JAKEMAN's footwear and force can be used.

46. ROBERTS, an adult female, is walking along a lane and sees a gated doorway which is the entrance to the rear garden of a large house. She is a bit hungry after her walk and thinks there may be some fruit she could eat within the garden walls. She enters the garden (as a trespasser) and she can see there is an array of raspberry bushes in fruit further up the garden. As ROBERTS walks up the garden, she sees a young man CORBETT sunbathing in his shorts; ROBERTS changes her mind about the fruit and approaches him with the intention of sexually touching him in the genital area of his shorts for a joke. When she gets closer, a large dog barks and awakes CORBETT and ROBERTS runs out of the garden.

Does ROBERTS commit the offence of trespass with intent to commit a relevant sexual offence (contrary to s. 63 of the Sexual Offences Act 2003)?

A Yes, but only if she actually carried out her intentions to touch CORBETT whilst she is a trespasser.

B No, ROBERTS does not commit the offence as the garden is not premises for the purposes of s. 63.

C Yes, ROBERTS commits the offence as the intent to commit a relevant sexual offence can come about after entry as a trespasser and a garden is premises for the purposes of s. 63.

D No, ROBERTS does not commit the offence because the intent for the relevant sexual offence needs to be formed before entry to the premises as a trespasser.

47. KNUL and BURT (two ordinary members of the public) are standing on a street corner when they are approached by PC CHETTY. PC CHETTY is making enquiries into an offence of burglary at a nearby warehouse and was told by the owner of the warehouse that KNUL and BURT are always hanging around the area and might have seen something. PC CHETTY asks KNUL if he knows anything about the burglary—at this point BURT advises KNUL not to answer any of the officer's questions as he will end up getting involved in something that is none of his business. KNUL remains silent and smirks at the officer. PC CHETTY turns to BURT and asks *'Well, you seem to know a lot. Do you know anything about this burglary then?'* BURT replies, *'Piss off! We don't have to answer any of your questions, you fuckin' pig!'*

At what stage, if at all, is the offence of obstruct police (contrary to s. 89(2) of the Police Act 1996) first committed?

A When BURT advises KNUL not to answer any questions put to him by PC CHETTY.

B When KNUL remains silent in response to the question posed to him by PC CHETTY.

C When BURT is abusive towards the officer and tells the officer *'We don't have to answer any of your questions'*.

D The offence has not been committed by BURT or KNUL.

48. CRANSHAW and GUBBIN work for a large insurance company. CRANSHAW supervises GUBBIN but the two do not get on at all resulting in several heated disagreements. GUBBIN wants to punish CRANSHAW and knows that CRANSHAW has her lunch in a nearby pub each day. He has a chat with POLLOCK (his friend) and encourages POLLOCK to assault CRANSHAW in the pub as a favour to him. POLLOCK agrees and GUBBIN provides a description of CRANSHAW to POLLOCK. POLLOCK goes into the pub, sees CRANSHAW and punches her in the face causing her injury. POLLOCK aims another punch at CRANSHAW who ducks out of the way causing POLLOCK to strike and injure BUTTON who is an innocent bystander. On his way out of the pub, POLLOCK sees EDGE who he has had personal disagreements with and he attacks EDGE causing EDGE serious injury.

Considering the liability of GUBBIN and the doctrine of transferred *mens rea*, which of the following comments is correct?

   A GUBBIN would be liable for the assault injuries to CRANSHAW alone.
   B GUBBIN would be liable for the assault injuries to CRANSHAW and BUTTON but not for the assault injuries sustained by EDGE.
   C GUBBIN would be liable for the assault injuries to CRANSHAW and EDGE but not for the assault injuries sustained by BUTTON.
   D GUBBIN would be liable for the assault injuries sustained by CRANSHAW, BUTTON and EDGE.

49. BARON is staying at his friend's address whilst his friend is on holiday. BARON has full use of the house and is allowed to bring his friend, STRETTON, to the house if he wishes. BARON and STRETTON are in the lounge of the house watching a football match between their team and their fierce local rivals in the FA Cup. During the match a defender from the team BARON and STRETTON support makes a mistake allowing the opposition to score a goal. The defender who made the error is a black male and BARON shouts out *'You stupid black bastard; fuck off home to your mud hut'*. This is shouted so loud that a number of people standing at a bus stop outside the house hear what is said and are extremely offended. BARON's intention is to stir up racial hatred in STRETTON and he had no idea that his comments could be heard outside the house.

In relation to using of words or behaviour or display of written materials (contrary to s. 18 of the Public Order Act 1986) does BARON commit an offence?

   A Yes, he commits the offence and in these circumstances would not have a defence.
   B No, as s. 18 only applies to activities carried out in a public place not a private dwelling.
   C No, because he intended to stir up racial hatred in STRETTON who was also in the same dwelling.
   D Yes, he commits the offence but would have a defence available if he can prove he was inside a dwelling and had no reason to believe that his words would be heard by a person outside that or any other dwelling.

50. PCs SUTTER and HANNON are discussing the Criminal Attempts Act 1981 with regards to their revision programme for their forthcoming examination. They are confused about this legislation. PC SUTTER makes the following statements to test HANNON's knowledge.

With regards to the Criminal Attempts Act 1981, which of the following statements made by PC SUTTER is correct?

A A person can be guilty of attempting low-value theft, even though it is triable summarily.

B A person can be found guilty of attempting to assist an offender contrary to s. 4 of the Criminal Law Act 1967.

C A person cannot be found guilty for attempting an offence, if it is impossible to commit the offence.

D A person who attempts an offence that is triable only on indictment can be tried either way.

51. WILLIS is walking from the train carrying a metal briefcase; the briefcase contains documents and his laptop. WILLIS is unaware that he is being followed by LAMBERT. WILLIS cuts through a car park followed closely by LAMBERT. LAMBERT removes a lump hammer from his coat and, from behind, strikes the metal briefcase with the hammer violently intending to steal the briefcase. The handle of the briefcase remains in WILLIS's hand but the briefcase falls to the ground; this is what LAMBERT intended. LAMBERT picks up the briefcase and makes good his escape.

Does LAMBERT commit the offence of robbery (contrary to s. 8 of the Theft Act 1968)?

A No, because WILLIS was not put in fear of the use of force, prior to the theft.

B Yes, force can be used against a person's property for an offence of robbery.

C No, because the force was not directly used on WILLIS.

D Yes, but you would need to prove some physical injury to WILLIS from the actions of LAMBERT.

52. PC ARROW is directed to attend a call where it is reported that a person is behaving suspiciously around some farm buildings. The officer arrives at the scene and sees PURLEY walking out of a farm building and across a field. There is a very large sign next to the field indicating that it is private property. As PURLEY climbs over a fence and into the road, PC ARROW stops him. PURLEY admits he was looking for somewhere to sleep for the night and was trespassing. The officer searches PURLEY and finds an air pistol in his possession. PC ARROW arrests PURLEY in respect of his commission of an offence of trespassing with a firearm on land (contrary to s. 20(2) of the Firearms Act 1968 and using the provisions of s. 24 of the Police and Criminal Evidence Act 1984). PC ARROW now wishes to use the provisions of s. 32 of the Police and Criminal Evidence Act 1984 to search PURLEY and the nearby farm building.

With regard to the officer's powers under s. 32 of the Police and Criminal Evidence Act 1984, which of the following comments is true?

A If PC ARROW suspects that PURLEY may present a danger to himself or others then he may search him.

B PC ARROW has a power under s. 32 to search PURLEY for evidence but only for evidence specifically relating to the offence for which he was arrested.

C PC ARROW may require PURLEY to remove his outer coat, jacket and gloves for the purpose of the search but he could not search in PURLEY's mouth.

D PC ARROW cannot search the farm building that PURLEY was seen walking out from under s. 32 of the Act.

53. MYLO is in his local village pub when a stranger to the village, TIMPSON, comes into the pub, buys a beer and sits down. After a short time MYLO engages TIMPSON in conversation. MYLO says to TIMPSON, *'I have some cannabis resin in my car, would you like some?'* MYLO has no drugs, he just sees TIMPSON as an easy target, but MYLO has some cubes of old chocolate in his car which in the dark would pass as cannabis resin. TIMPSON says that he is interested and enquires into the cost. MYLO states that a small cube as it is good stuff will be £20. MYLO gets up from his seat when the local PCSO comes into the pub to speak to the licensee about an unconnected matter. In view of this, MYLO says to TIMPSON that the offer is off and leaves the pub.

Considering the offence of supplying a controlled drug (contrary to s. 4 of the Misuse of Drugs Act 1971), does MYLO commit an offence?

A No, he does not commit the offence as he withdrew the offer to supply.

B Yes, he commits the offence as soon as he makes the offer to supply to TIMPSON.

C No, he does not commit the offence as he was in possession of chocolate not cannabis.

D Yes, he commits the offence when the price is agreed for the supplying of the drug.

54. SIMPSON is a civilian authorised investigating officer and is dealing with TAYLOR for offences of burglary other building; TAYLOR has been stealing power tools and lawn mowers from garden sheds. SIMPSON will be interviewing TAYLOR on her own. From the file it is evident that if TAYLOR fails to answer certain questions there would be a potential to give him a special warning (under s. 36 of the Criminal Justice and Public Order Act 1994).

With regard to authorised investigators, which of the following statements is correct in relation to SIMPSON's powers to give a special warning in an interview?

A Civilian investigators cannot give a special warning.
B Civilian investigators can only give a special warning if they interview a suspect in the company of a police officer.
C Civilian investigators can give a special warning, but need a police officer to warn the suspect of the inference a court may draw from their silence.
D Civilian investigators can give a special warning and also warn the suspect of the inference a court may draw from their silence.

55. WILSON is standing surety of £5,000 to secure the attendance on bail to the court of JONES for offences of burglary. WILSON has found out from a friend that JONES is making plans to leave the area and will not attend court. WILSON believes that JONES will not appear and wishes to relinquish his surety for securing JONES's attendance.

To comply with the Bail Act 1976, as he believes JONES will not attend court, which of the following is correct in order that WILSON can be relieved of his obligation as a surety?

A WILSON must attend the police station where bail was granted and inform any custody sergeant of his wish to be removed as a surety.
B WILSON must attend the police station where bail was granted and inform any constable of his wish to be removed as a surety.
C WILSON must notify a constable in writing that JONES is unlikely to surrender to custody and for that reason he wishes to be relieved of his obligations as a surety.
D WILSON must notify the custody sergeant (in writing) who granted bail to JONES that JONES is unlikely to surrender to custody and for that reason he wishes to be relieved of his obligations as a surety.

56. FOSTER, an adult female, has just been out for her morning run. She is wearing pants, shorts, bra and a vest top. On her arrival home, her friend CLAY has come round to have a coffee with her. FOSTER has cramps from her run and asks CLAY to massage her. CLAY agrees and gets a small rolling pin from the kitchen drawer. FOSTER lies face down on the settee; CLAY then proceeds to roll the rolling pin up and down FOSTER's back. CLAY then uses the rolling pin to massage FOSTER's inner thigh and runs the rolling pin several times over FOSTER's buttocks. CLAY then asks FOSTER to remove her vest top and bra and massages her naked back with the rolling pin. CLAY requests FOSTER to turn over, which exposes her breasts and CLAY using her hands then fondles FOSTER's breasts.

Considering the legislation under the Sexual Offences Act 2003, when does 'touching' first take place?

A When CLAY fondles FOSTER's breasts.
B When CLAY massages FOSTER by using the rolling pin on her naked back.
C When CLAY massages FOSTER by using the rolling pin on her buttocks.
D When CLAY first massages FOSTER's back with the rolling pin.

57. GRANT works in the local travel agents in a large shopping centre and her manager is AZIZ. AZIZ fancies GRANT but he knows this is not reciprocated. AZIZ decides that he is going to kidnap GRANT; he knows from working with GRANT that she loves fast flashy cars. He texts her from the underground car park of the shopping centre and lies to her that he has come to work in his brother's Ferrari and would she like to go for a ride. GRANT cannot resist the temptation and goes to the underground car park. On arrival there, there is no Ferrari but a large van. AZIZ jumps out of the van, takes hold of GRANT and throws her into the back of the van, binds her with rope and then drives off.

Considering the offence at common law, when does AZIZ first commit the offence of kidnap?

A AZIZ first commits kidnap when he throws her into the back of the van.
B AZIZ first commits kidnap when he sends her the text.
C AZIZ first commits kidnap when she walks from her desk to the car park.
D AZIZ first commits kidnap when he drives off.

58. CATO (aged 17) is involved in a car accident and is rushed to the accident and emergency ward of a nearby hospital for treatment. CATO has suffered significant harm as a consequence of being involved in the accident and is receiving treatment for his injuries when his parents arrive. CATO's parents are adamant that they do not want CATO to stay at the hospital as a relative of theirs has recently died in hospital having been admitted for a minor operation and then contracting the MRSA 'superbug'. CATO's parents are causing a disturbance at the hospital, demanding that they be allowed to take their son away and treat him at their home. The police are called to the incident and PC BUCKINGHAM attends the incident.

With regard to police powers under s. 46 of the Children Act 1989, which of the following comments is true?

A The powers under s. 46 cannot be used by the officer as CATO is 17 years old.

B If PC BUCKINGHAM has reasonable cause to believe that CATO would otherwise be likely to suffer serious harm, he may take such steps as are reasonable to prevent CATO being removed from the hospital.

C PC BUCKINGHAM can take such steps as are reasonable to prevent CATO's removal from the hospital if he has the authority of an officer of at least the rank of inspector to do so.

D If PC BUCKINGHAM reasonably believes that the continued presence of CATO's parents may result in serious harm to CATO, he can remove the parents from the hospital premises.

59. FELL (who is 18 years old) and SAYER (who is 17 years old) have been arrested in connection with an offence of robbery. The officer in charge of the case, DC HEINZMAN, has information and evidence that FELL and SAYER are responsible for a large number of other robbery offences and wishes to speak to them about these offences. As such, DC HEINZMAN seeks to have FELL and SAYER remanded into police custody under s. 128 of the Magistrates' Courts Act 1980 so that he can speak to them about the other robbery offences.

Which of the following comments is correct in relation to such a remand?

A FELL could be remanded in police custody for a period not exceeding three clear days; SAYER could be remanded in police custody for a period not exceeding 24 hours.

B FELL could be remanded in police custody for a period not exceeding three clear days; SAYER could not be remanded in police custody as he is a juvenile.

C FELL and SAYER could be remanded in police custody for a period not exceeding three clear days.

D FELL and SAYER could be remanded in police custody for a period not exceeding 24 hours.

60. FIELD is a 12-year-old girl and is attracted to her piano teacher McNULTY who provides private tuition to FIELD at his home address. For some time FIELD's mother accompanied her to her lessons; however, as FIELD has been having lessons for three years with McNULTY her mother now allows her to go on her own. FIELD is physically well developed for her age, however McNULTY is aware of her true age. During a piano lesson FIELD asks McNULTY to touch her legs up to her pants. McNULTY flatly refuses and tells her not to be so silly. FIELD says to McNULTY, *'Well, I really want you to have sex with me, to be my first'*. At this, she stands up and removes her pants; McNULTY, shocked and worried, leaves the room immediately.

Considering s. 44 of the Serious Crime Act 2007 (intentionally encouraging or assisting an offence), is FIELD liable?

A FIELD is not guilty in these circumstances as rape would be committed if McNULTY had sex with her, which is for her own protection.

B FIELD does commit the offence as she is over the age of 10 years, the age of criminal responsibility.

C FIELD is not guilty in these circumstances as the act she encouraged did not take place.

D FIELD is guilty of the offence but in the circumstances it would be an attempt owing to her age being under 13.

61. The Sexual Offences (Amendment) Act 1992 allows the victim anonymity in sexual offence cases.

In relation to this legislation, which of the following statements is correct regarding offences of sexual assault by touching?

A The victim is entitled to anonymity until the end of the trial or any appeal.

B The victim is entitled to anonymity indefinitely.

C The victim is entitled to anonymity throughout their lifetime.

D Anonymity does not apply to the offence of sexual assault by touching.

62. David HOWE and Jane HOWE are husband and wife and have separated after David found out that Jane was having an affair. Whilst they arrange the sale of the matrimonial home to split the proceeds, Jane is living in the matrimonial home and David is renting a flat. The situation between the two has deteriorated and they are arguing over who owns what in the matrimonial home. One evening, whilst Jane is out, David visits the matrimonial home with his friend FISHER. They force the front door of the house and remove several items of property, including a fridge and a television, from the house. David HOWE is convinced that he has every right to the property as he paid for it and FISHER believes that he is helping David exercise a lawful right. Whilst FISHER is outside the house loading the van they drove to the house in, David HOWE sees a watch that he knows belongs to Jane and decides to take it for revenge and leaves the house.

Which of the following statements is correct in respect of the law relating to the Theft Act 1968?

A David HOWE could be charged with theft (s. 1) in relation to the watch but such a prosecution may only be instituted against him with the consent of the Director of Public Prosecutions.

B FISHER has committed an offence of burglary (s. 9(1)(a)) when he enters the house with David HOWE.

C David HOWE could be charged with burglary (s. 9(1)(b)) of the watch.

D No offence under the Theft Act has been committed by either man in this situation.

63. MILES is walking in the red light area of the city because he is considering paying for the services of a prostitute. On one of the street corners he sees CALDERSHAW, a prostitute, plying her trade. MILES realises that he has come out of the house with no cash so he decides to rape CALDERSHAW instead. MILES punches CALDERSHAW in the face and she falls to the ground and he can see clearly that she has no pants on. However, out of the top pocket of her denim jacket a large amount of cash falls to the ground near to her. MILES changes his mind, picks up the cash and runs off. A short time later he sees NOWAKOWSKI looking into a shop window and he can see her purse sticking out of her handbag so he decides to steal it. MILES places his hand on the purse and picks it out of her handbag, of which NOWAKOWSKI is totally unaware. At that moment a person behind MILES accidentally bumps into him and in turn he accidentally pushes NOWAKOWSKI into the shop window causing a deep wound to her face. MILES makes good his escape.

Considering only the offence of robbery (contrary to s. 8 of the Theft Act 1968), which of the following statements is correct?

A MILES commits robbery only with regards to CALDERSHAW.

B MILES commits robbery only with regard to NOWAKOWSKI.

C MILES commits robbery against both CALDERSHAW and NOWAKOWSKI.

D MILES does not commit any robbery offence.

64. MONROE is being investigated for child sexual offences. MONROE has been interviewed about some of the offences that are known but there is further investigation needed before a decision to charge can be made. DC HARRIS wants the bail extension from the initial period of 28 days to three months owing to the complexities of the case.

If all the conditions required are met, what is the rank of the officer that can authorise this extension?

A An officer of superintendent rank or above.
B An officer of the rank of chief inspector or above who is not involved in the case.
C An officer of the rank of inspector or above.
D An officer of the rank of inspector or above who is not involved in the case.

65. MICHAM has been arrested in relation to an offence of robbery. He denies any involvement in the offence, disputing the identification evidence. MICHAM has indicated that he will not take part in any video identification or identification parade so consideration is being given to a group identification process.

Considering Annex C of Code D of the Codes of Practice (dealing with group identification), which of the following statements is correct?

A A group identification may only take place with MITCHAM's consent and cooperation.
B A group identification process can take place at a police station.
C A group identification process must involve a moving (not stationary) group.
D A group identification process must be video recorded in all circumstances.

66. PC VICKERS and PC MOORE attend 25 Trent Street, the dwelling of Henry SEARS who is suspected of a street robbery that occurred this morning. The officers wish to search the house to see if he has returned home. Joan SEARS, his mother who rents the address with her son, gives consent for the officers to search the house for Henry. PC VICKERS and PC MOORE search the living room and then the kitchen. In the walk-in pantry, the officers see in the corner a box of mobile phones and believing that these maybe the subject of a theft the officers seize them. As the officers seize the phones, Joan says to the officers *'Fuck off'*; however, they continue to search and in Henry's bedroom find a blank credit card on the window sill and seize them. Joan then says to the officers *'Henry is not here, you must leave now.'* The officers then leave the house.

Which of the following statements is correct with regard to the actions of PC VICKERS and PC MOORE?

A The officers had no power to seize the phones or the credit card as they were searching for Henry SEARS.
B The officers could seize the mobile phones but not the credit card because when told to 'Fuck off' they were then trespassing and should have left the dwelling.
C The officers had no power to enter or search the dwelling in these circumstances even with consent, as they would need a premises warrant.
D The officers' actions were correct as they had permission to enter and search; they can seize property unconnected to the original offence with consent and 'Fuck off' is not classed as a full removal of permission to remain lawfully.

67. CALLAGHAN drives onto the forecourt of a motorway service station and whilst filling his car with fuel sees RICE, a hitchhiker, holding a sign stating 'Lift to London?' CALLAGHAN is attracted to RICE and approaches her and states he will give her a lift. RICE accepts and gets in to the front passenger seat of CALLAGHAN's car. CALLAGHAN drives off the forecourt onto the motorway. The two engage in conversation as CALLAGHAN drives along the slip road towards the motorway and just before the vehicle joins the motorway CALLAGHAN tells RICE *'Now I've got you, I'm going to fuck you whether you like it or not!'* and grabs hold of RICE's right breast. RICE is petrified and thinks she is going to be raped. She opens the passenger door and jumps out of the vehicle, breaking her arm as she hits the surface of the road.

Considering the legal concepts regarding an intervening act, which of the comments below is correct?

   A CALLAGHAN cannot be held responsible for the actions of RICE which result in her injury as he did not directly inflict them.
   B CALLAGHAN can be held liable for the injury caused to RICE if a court considers her actions might reasonably have been anticipated in such a situation.
   C CALLAGHAN could only be held liable for the injuries to RICE if he considered they might take place as a result of his actions.
   D CALLAGHAN cannot be held responsible for the injuries caused to RICE as RICE brought them about of her own volition (opening the car door and jumping out of the vehicle).

68. BANKS is an adult male and he falsely imprisons both WEST, an adult male, and CARTER, an adult female. BANKS has lured them to his house on the pretext that he is thinking of selling the property knowing that they are both interested in buying his house with their respective partners. BANKS locks all the doors to the property and produces a large sword. Both WEST and CARTER are very scared and when he requests that they both remove their clothes they do so. BANKS then tells WEST to put his penis into CARTER's mouth and insert his fingers in her vagina. Initially WEST refuses but after threats with the sword both WEST and CARTER submit to BANKS's requests.

Considering only offences contrary to the Sexual Offences Act 2003, which of the statements below is correct with regards to the criminal responsibility of all parties?

   A BANKS commits an offence of causing sexual activity without consent and WEST commits two offences of rape.
   B BANKS would be guilty of causing sexual activity without consent if it could be shown that it was for sexual gratification.
   C BANKS commits the offence of causing sexual activity without consent.
   D BANKS commits causing sexual activity without consent and WEST commits rape and assault by penetration.

69. RUTTER is having problems with her boss PATTERSON who has put her on an action plan to improve RUTTER's professional skills. RUTTER believes this is unjustified, which it is not, and therefore decides to cause PATTERSON anxiety or distress. RUTTER sends PATTERSON a false letter from a solicitor stating that PATTERSON is being taken to court by a nearby neighbour for the noise her dog makes in the garden in the morning. RUTTER also sends a text from an unidentified mobile phone stating that PATTERSON's daughter has been involved in a minor accident at school. RUTTER also puts dog faeces through PATTERSON's letterbox.

Considering the offences under s. 1(1) of the Malicious Communications Act 1988, which, if any, offences have been committed?

A None of the acts by RUTTER are covered by this legislation.
B RUTTER only commits the offence when she sends the false letter.
C RUTTER only commits the offence when she sends the false letter and the text.
D RUTTER commits the offence on all three occasions.

70. POTOLI and VERRITT are civil partners who have been having problems with ROSS (who frequents a pub that POTOLI and VERRITT visit). ROSS constantly directs abuse at POTOLI and VERRITT about their sexuality and the pair have had enough. They decide that ROSS needs to be taught a lesson and agree that they will attack him (although they do not intend to cause him any more than very minor harm, i.e. a common battery). The two plan the offence so that there will be no witnesses and so that ROSS will not be able to identify them as the offenders. On the night of the planned offence, they leave their house and wait for ROSS in an alleyway at the side of the pub. Whilst waiting, POTOLI has second thoughts about committing the offence and tells VERRITT that he does not want to go through with their plan. VERRITT states that he understands and that they should forget their plan. The two men return to their home and ROSS is not subject to any harm by the pair. As it turns out, ROSS could not possibly have been assaulted as he was not drinking in the pub that evening—he was on holiday in Poland.

Considering only the offence of statutory conspiracy (contrary to s. 1 of the Criminal Law Act 1977), which of the following comments is correct?

A A conspiracy offence does not exist as you can only conspire to commit an indictable offence and an offence of 'common battery' under s. 39 of the Criminal Justice Act 1988 is an offence that is triable summarily.
B A conspiracy offence has not been committed as there was never any 'end product' as a consequence of the agreement between the two men.
C A conspiracy offence has not been committed as it was impossible for ROSS to be assaulted as he was in Poland at the time the two men planned to assault him.
D No conspiracy offence has been committed as the two participants are civil partners.

71. PUGH is owed £200 by CANNON. PUGH has spoken to CANNON about the debt on several occasions but there is no sign of CANNON paying the money back. PUGH has become frustrated by this situation and decides that enough is enough and the next time he sees CANNON he will get his money. He sees CANNON walking along a street and confronts him demanding that the debt be repaid. CANNON becomes annoyed and tells PUGH he will never repay the money. PUGH produces a knife and holds it to CANNON's face and tells him that unless he pays the debt he will be stabbed. PUGH knows the means he is using to get the debt repaid is wrong but believes he has a lawful right to have the debt repaid. CANNON refuses, so PUGH cuts CANNON across the face to encourage him to pay up. CANNON panics and hands over £200 from his wallet to PUGH as settlement for the debt. Satisfied that the debt has been settled, PUGH walks away.

At what point, if at all, has the offence of robbery been committed?

A The offence of robbery has not been committed in these circumstances.
B When PUGH produces the knife and holds it to CANNON's face.
C When PUGH uses the knife to cut CANNON across his face.
D When CANNON hands the £200 to PUGH.

72. POPESCU, an adult male, has been arrested for several offences of burglary and you intend to search properties that may have evidence relating to the offences that POPESCU has been arrested for. POPESCU occupies a house at 22 Cross Avenue, which he rents from the estate agents Manning and Sons and he also owns and controls a lock-up garage which he uses to keep his car in. You have intelligence at your disposal which indicates POPESCU rents a storage facility in a warehouse but this is unconfirmed and you only reasonably suspect he controls the storage facility..

With the correct authorisation from an inspector or above, which of the following statements is correct as to which properties can be searched by a constable under s. 18 of PACE 1984?

A All three properties can be searched.
B The storage facility and the house he rents.
C The house he rents and his garage.
D Only the house he rents.

73. MIFFLIN is a hypochondriac and believes that she has a serious condition which is causing her a great deal of pain (this is not true). She visits her local surgery and speaks with her general practitioner, Dr PATTEN, and asks for a pain-killing injection to ease her suffering. Dr PATTEN refuses the injection as he is aware of MIFFLIN's hypochondria and knows that she is not in any pain. MIFFLIN tells Dr PATTEN that if he does not provide her with the pain-killing injection, she will leave the surgery and slash all the tyres on his expensive sports car which is parked directly outside the surgery. Dr PATTEN believes MIFFLIN and provides her with the pain-killing injection.

Which of the following is true?

A This is not a case of blackmail as there has been no 'gain' or 'loss' in property.
B The offence of blackmail is committed at the moment MIFFLIN makes the demand for the pain-killing injection accompanied by the threats to damage Dr PATTEN's car.
C This is not a case of blackmail as the menaces were not threatened 'then and there'; the damage was going to take place at another time and in another place.
D The offence of blackmail is committed at the moment Dr PATTEN provides the pain-killing injection to MIFFLIN.

74. PC VERRIN arrests WATERFIELD for failing to take part in a preliminary screening test (for the purposes of drink/drive offences under the Road Traffic Act 1988). Unfortunately, the arrest was unlawful as PC VERRIN was a trespasser on land owned by WATERFIELD when the arrest was made. After the arrest, PC VERRIN takes hold of WATERFIELD and a struggle ensues during which PC VERRIN is assaulted by WATERFIELD resulting in PC VERRIN sustaining several small cuts and bruises to his left arm. Other officers arrive at the scene and WATERFIELD is escorted to a designated police station where he is brought in to the custody block and placed in front of the custody officer, PS BLACKBURN. When PS BLACKBURN asks WATERFIELD for his name, WATERFIELD responds by telling the officer to *'Fuck off'* and punching PS BLACKBURN in the face, causing minor bruising to PS BLACKBURN's face.

Has an offence of assault police (contrary to s. 89(1) of the Police Act 1996) been committed?

A No, the arrest made by PC VERRIN was unlawful. This means that any action by the police following an unlawful arrest (including that of the custody officer) cannot be regarded as that of an officer carrying out the lawful execution of his/her duty.
B Yes, the offence has been committed upon PC VERRIN and PS BLACKBURN.
C No, as the injuries received by both officers are minor.
D Yes, but only upon PS BLACKBURN.

75. NELSON is an 18-year-old male and his new girlfriend is LENNON, a 15-year-old female (NELSON is aware of LENNON's age). They have been going out together for a couple of weeks. LENNON is very shy and knows very little about sex. NELSON decides that the only way he is going to be able to have sex with LENNON is to show her pictures of a pornographic nature to lower her inhibitions so he can achieve sexual gratification at a later date. NELSON at first shows LENNON cartoon still images of persons having sexual intercourse. Then a day later he shows her moving cartoons of persons having sexual intercourse. A week later as LENNON is now showing more interest, NELSON shows her a pornographic video involving sexual intercourse between males and females via the internet. NELSON believes that after this showing she will have sex with him. LENNON is not amused by this and tells him their relationship is over.

Considering the offence under s. 12 of the Sexual Offences Act 2003 (causing a child to watch a sex act) when if at all does NELSON first commit the offence?

A NELSON does not commit the offence as no sexual gratification was obtained whilst LENNON was exposed to the pornography.
B NELSON commits the offence when he showed her the internet pornography as that was when he believed he would obtain sexual gratification.
C NELSON commits the offence when he shows the moving cartoon pornography.
D NELSON commits the offence when he shows LENNON the first pornographic cartoon still image.

76. Under s. 33 of the Criminal Justice and Police Act 2001, a court is empowered to give an offender a travel restriction order for a drug trafficking offence. This is to prohibit them leaving the United Kingdom after their release from prison. They are guilty of an offence if they do not comply and they may have to surrender their passport.

Under s. 33 of the Criminal Justice and Police Act 2001, which of the following statements is the criteria for the court issuing such an order for a drug trafficking offender?

A Must have had a sentence imposed of at least three years, and then the restriction order is for a minimum of two years.
B Must have had a sentence imposed of at least four years, and then the restriction order is for a minimum of two years.
C Must have had a sentence imposed of at least three years, and then the restriction order is for a minimum of three years.
D Must have had a sentence imposed of at least four years, and then the restriction order is for a minimum of three years.

77. PC HEWITT is a uniformed officer on foot patrol in his neighbourhood area; he is fully equipped with utility belt and CS spray. During his morning shift, he is sent to a report of persons acting suspiciously at the rear of a house. On arrival, HEWITT goes round to the rear of the house and he can see a large amount of cash on the kitchen table. HEWITT finds that the rear of the property is secure and he returns to the front of the house. He tries the front door and it is insecure and it opens. He enters the hallway of the house and announces himself to see if anybody is in the house and to ensure everything is alright. There is no reply and it is obvious that nobody is in. HEWITT has a large debt from gambling and he decides that he is going to steal the cash from the kitchen table. He then enters the kitchen from the hallway and puts the cash inside his clothing and leaves the premises.

Considering offences of burglary under the Theft Act 1968, which of the following statements is correct?

A HEWITT commits burglary contrary to s. 9(1)(a) of the Theft Act 1968 when he decides to steal the money from the kitchen.

B HEWITT commits burglary contrary to s. 9(1)(a) of the Theft Act 1968 when he enters the kitchen from the hallway and steals the cash.

C HEWITT commits aggravated burglary contrary to s. 10 of the Theft Act 1968 when he enters the kitchen from the hallway and steals the cash.

D HEWITT would be guilty of theft contrary to s. 1 of the Theft Act 1968.

78. CHIVERTON needs money to buy drugs and decides to target Jewish people to steal from as he hates Jews and, as far is he is concerned, they are all rich and have money to spare. He waits outside a synagogue and sees NASH leave the synagogue and walk towards his car. As NASH was seen leaving the synagogue, CHIVERTON automatically presumes that he is Jewish although this is not the case; NASH is a Christian and was actually visiting the synagogue to speak to a friend. CHIVERTON sneaks up behind NASH and steals his wallet. NASH felt the wallet being taken and turns around to confront CHIVERTON, demanding that he hand the wallet back. CHIVERTON runs away from NASH who chases after CHIVERTON. Several minutes later, with NASH still pursuing him, CHIVERTON stops, turns around and, in order to escape, punches NASH in the face causing bruising to NASH's left cheek. NASH falls to the floor and CHIVERTON says, 'Have some of that, you Jewish tosser!'

Thinking about the law in relation to racially and religiously aggravated offences (as per the Crime and Disorder Act 1998), which of the following comments is correct?

A CHIVERTON could be charged with an offence of religiously aggravated theft (s. 1 of the Theft Act 1968) in these circumstances.

B CHIVERTON could be charged with an offence of religiously aggravated battery (s. 39 of the Criminal Justice Act 1988) in these circumstances.

C CHIVERTON could be charged with an offence of religiously aggravated robbery (s. 8 of the Theft Act 1968) in these circumstances.

D A variety of offences have been committed by CHIVERTON but none of them are religiously aggravated.

79. DC HOLTOM is putting a file together in relation to a case of rape where the offender has pleaded 'not guilty' and the case is going to be heard in Crown Court. The officer is being assisted by TI SINGH. TI SINGH asks a number of questions about the evidence in the case particularly relating to its weight and admissibility in court. The officers disagree on several elements of this area of law and their supervisor, DS RABY steps in to correct their misunderstanding.

Considering the issues in relation to the weight and admissibility of evidence, which of the following comments is correct?

A TI SINGH states evidence can be excluded if its prejudicial effect outweighs its probative value.

B DC HOLTOM states that the question of admissibility of evidence is a question of fact to be decided by members of a jury.

C TI SINGH states that evidence cannot be excluded based on the incompetence of a witness.

D DC HOLTOM states that evidence can only be excluded via the use of s. 76 of the Police and Criminal Evidence Act 1984.

80. It is an offence under s. 33A of the Sexual Offences Act 1956 to keep a brothel, manage such premises or to act or assist in the management of a brothel.

Which of the following statements is correct with regards to the number/s of prostitute/s on the premises being managed for the offence to be committed?

A Only one prostitute is required.

B More than one prostitute.

C More than two prostitutes.

D More than three prostitutes.

Answer Sheet

1 ⊏A⊐ ⊏B⊐ ⊏C⊐ ⊏D⊐	31 ⊏A⊐ ⊏B⊐ ⊏C⊐ ⊏D⊐	61 ⊏A⊐ ⊏B⊐ ⊏C⊐ ⊏D⊐
2 ⊏A⊐ ⊏B⊐ ⊏C⊐ ⊏D⊐	32 ⊏A⊐ ⊏B⊐ ⊏C⊐ ⊏D⊐	62 ⊏A⊐ ⊏B⊐ ⊏C⊐ ⊏D⊐
3 ⊏A⊐ ⊏B⊐ ⊏C⊐ ⊏D⊐	33 ⊏A⊐ ⊏B⊐ ⊏C⊐ ⊏D⊐	63 ⊏A⊐ ⊏B⊐ ⊏C⊐ ⊏D⊐
4 ⊏A⊐ ⊏B⊐ ⊏C⊐ ⊏D⊐	34 ⊏A⊐ ⊏B⊐ ⊏C⊐ ⊏D⊐	64 ⊏A⊐ ⊏B⊐ ⊏C⊐ ⊏D⊐
5 ⊏A⊐ ⊏B⊐ ⊏C⊐ ⊏D⊐	35 ⊏A⊐ ⊏B⊐ ⊏C⊐ ⊏D⊐	65 ⊏A⊐ ⊏B⊐ ⊏C⊐ ⊏D⊐
6 ⊏A⊐ ⊏B⊐ ⊏C⊐ ⊏D⊐	36 ⊏A⊐ ⊏B⊐ ⊏C⊐ ⊏D⊐	66 ⊏A⊐ ⊏B⊐ ⊏C⊐ ⊏D⊐
7 ⊏A⊐ ⊏B⊐ ⊏C⊐ ⊏D⊐	37 ⊏A⊐ ⊏B⊐ ⊏C⊐ ⊏D⊐	67 ⊏A⊐ ⊏B⊐ ⊏C⊐ ⊏D⊐
8 ⊏A⊐ ⊏B⊐ ⊏C⊐ ⊏D⊐	38 ⊏A⊐ ⊏B⊐ ⊏C⊐ ⊏D⊐	68 ⊏A⊐ ⊏B⊐ ⊏C⊐ ⊏D⊐
9 ⊏A⊐ ⊏B⊐ ⊏C⊐ ⊏D⊐	39 ⊏A⊐ ⊏B⊐ ⊏C⊐ ⊏D⊐	69 ⊏A⊐ ⊏B⊐ ⊏C⊐ ⊏D⊐
10 ⊏A⊐ ⊏B⊐ ⊏C⊐ ⊏D⊐	40 ⊏A⊐ ⊏B⊐ ⊏C⊐ ⊏D⊐	70 ⊏A⊐ ⊏B⊐ ⊏C⊐ ⊏D⊐
11 ⊏A⊐ ⊏B⊐ ⊏C⊐ ⊏D⊐	41 ⊏A⊐ ⊏B⊐ ⊏C⊐ ⊏D⊐	71 ⊏A⊐ ⊏B⊐ ⊏C⊐ ⊏D⊐
12 ⊏A⊐ ⊏B⊐ ⊏C⊐ ⊏D⊐	42 ⊏A⊐ ⊏B⊐ ⊏C⊐ ⊏D⊐	72 ⊏A⊐ ⊏B⊐ ⊏C⊐ ⊏D⊐
13 ⊏A⊐ ⊏B⊐ ⊏C⊐ ⊏D⊐	43 ⊏A⊐ ⊏B⊐ ⊏C⊐ ⊏D⊐	73 ⊏A⊐ ⊏B⊐ ⊏C⊐ ⊏D⊐
14 ⊏A⊐ ⊏B⊐ ⊏C⊐ ⊏D⊐	44 ⊏A⊐ ⊏B⊐ ⊏C⊐ ⊏D⊐	74 ⊏A⊐ ⊏B⊐ ⊏C⊐ ⊏D⊐
15 ⊏A⊐ ⊏B⊐ ⊏C⊐ ⊏D⊐	45 ⊏A⊐ ⊏B⊐ ⊏C⊐ ⊏D⊐	75 ⊏A⊐ ⊏B⊐ ⊏C⊐ ⊏D⊐
16 ⊏A⊐ ⊏B⊐ ⊏C⊐ ⊏D⊐	46 ⊏A⊐ ⊏B⊐ ⊏C⊐ ⊏D⊐	76 ⊏A⊐ ⊏B⊐ ⊏C⊐ ⊏D⊐
17 ⊏A⊐ ⊏B⊐ ⊏C⊐ ⊏D⊐	47 ⊏A⊐ ⊏B⊐ ⊏C⊐ ⊏D⊐	77 ⊏A⊐ ⊏B⊐ ⊏C⊐ ⊏D⊐
18 ⊏A⊐ ⊏B⊐ ⊏C⊐ ⊏D⊐	48 ⊏A⊐ ⊏B⊐ ⊏C⊐ ⊏D⊐	78 ⊏A⊐ ⊏B⊐ ⊏C⊐ ⊏D⊐
19 ⊏A⊐ ⊏B⊐ ⊏C⊐ ⊏D⊐	49 ⊏A⊐ ⊏B⊐ ⊏C⊐ ⊏D⊐	79 ⊏A⊐ ⊏B⊐ ⊏C⊐ ⊏D⊐
20 ⊏A⊐ ⊏B⊐ ⊏C⊐ ⊏D⊐	50 ⊏A⊐ ⊏B⊐ ⊏C⊐ ⊏D⊐	80 ⊏A⊐ ⊏B⊐ ⊏C⊐ ⊏D⊐
21 ⊏A⊐ ⊏B⊐ ⊏C⊐ ⊏D⊐	51 ⊏A⊐ ⊏B⊐ ⊏C⊐ ⊏D⊐	
22 ⊏A⊐ ⊏B⊐ ⊏C⊐ ⊏D⊐	52 ⊏A⊐ ⊏B⊐ ⊏C⊐ ⊏D⊐	
23 ⊏A⊐ ⊏B⊐ ⊏C⊐ ⊏D⊐	53 ⊏A⊐ ⊏B⊐ ⊏C⊐ ⊏D⊐	
24 ⊏A⊐ ⊏B⊐ ⊏C⊐ ⊏D⊐	54 ⊏A⊐ ⊏B⊐ ⊏C⊐ ⊏D⊐	
25 ⊏A⊐ ⊏B⊐ ⊏C⊐ ⊏D⊐	55 ⊏A⊐ ⊏B⊐ ⊏C⊐ ⊏D⊐	
26 ⊏A⊐ ⊏B⊐ ⊏C⊐ ⊏D⊐	56 ⊏A⊐ ⊏B⊐ ⊏C⊐ ⊏D⊐	
27 ⊏A⊐ ⊏B⊐ ⊏C⊐ ⊏D⊐	57 ⊏A⊐ ⊏B⊐ ⊏C⊐ ⊏D⊐	
28 ⊏A⊐ ⊏B⊐ ⊏C⊐ ⊏D⊐	58 ⊏A⊐ ⊏B⊐ ⊏C⊐ ⊏D⊐	
29 ⊏A⊐ ⊏B⊐ ⊏C⊐ ⊏D⊐	59 ⊏A⊐ ⊏B⊐ ⊏C⊐ ⊏D⊐	
30 ⊏A⊐ ⊏B⊐ ⊏C⊐ ⊏D⊐	60 ⊏A⊐ ⊏B⊐ ⊏C⊐ ⊏D⊐	

Marking instructions

- Mark like this ⊏A⊐
- Make no stray marks
- Please do **NOT** tick, cross, or circle

OXFORD
UNIVERSITY PRESS

Blackstone's Police Investigators'
Mock Examination Paper 2019

Pack 2

Contents

DO NOT OPEN THIS ANSWER PACK UNTIL YOU HAVE COMPLETED THE MOCK EXAM

Blackstone's Police Investigators'
Mock Examination Paper 2019

Marking Instructions

Lay your answer sheet next to the marking matrix as shown; you may find it useful to fold the answer sheet to do this. Starting with Question 1, compare your marked answer (in the example this is 'C') with the correct answer given on the marking matrix. If the correct answer matches your marked answer put a '1' inside the white box on the relevant row. If it does not (see Question 2) put a '0'.

Please follow these instructions carefully to ensure accuracy. Marks ('1' or '0') should only be made in the white blank boxes (which indicate the subject area a question is related to)—please do not write anything in the grey boxes.

Question	Answer	General Principles and Police Powers	Serious Crime and other offences	Property Offences	Sexual Offences	Validation
1	C	1				
2	A			0		
3	B		1			
4	C				1	
5	A		0			
6	B			1		
7	D					1

1 ⊏A⊐ ⊏B⊐ ▬C▬ ⊏D⊐
2 ⊏A⊐ ▬B▬ ⊏C⊐ ⊏D⊐
3 ⊏A⊐ ▬B▬ ⊏C⊐ ⊏D⊐
4 ⊏A⊐ ⊏B⊐ ▬C▬ ⊏D⊐
5 ⊏A⊐ ⊏B⊐ ⊏C⊐ ▬D▬
6 ⊏A⊐ ▬B▬ ⊏C⊐ ⊏D⊐
7 ⊏A⊐ ⊏B⊐ ⊏C⊐ ▬D▬

When you have marked the first 30 questions, add up the total for each column (General Principles and Police Powers; Serious Crime and other offences; Property Offences; and Sexual Offences) and enter the totals into the boxes marked A1, B1, etc. Then transfer these totals into the corresponding box ('A1', 'B1', etc.) on the score sheet.

28	D			0		
29	B			1		
30	C					1
Totals		A1　5	B1　3	C1　4	D1　2	E1　2

					Total	
General Principles and Police Powers	A1	5	A2	A3	**Total** (out of 27) (= A1 + A2 + A3)	
Serious Crime and other offences	B1	3	B2	B3	**Total** (out of 17) (= B1 + B2 + B3)	
Property Offences	C1	4	C2	C3	**Total** (out of 14) (= C1 + C2 + C3)	
Sexual Offences	D1	2	D2	D3	**Total** (out of 12) (= D1 + D2 + D3)	
					Total questions right (out of 70)	

Then do the same for Questions 31 to 60 and fill in boxes A2 to D2 on the score sheet, and finally Questions 61 to 80, which will enable you to fill in boxes A3 to D3 on the score sheet.

Total up A1 + A2 + A3, which will give you a score for General Principles and Police Powers. Then do the same for Serious Crime and other offences, Property Offences, and Sexual Offences. You will then have a total for each subject area, which you can add up to reach a final total for the whole exam.

Compare your final total to the table underneath the score sheet, which will indicate whether or not you have passed the mock examination. The pass mark for the exam is 39.

Marking Matrix, Questions 1–30

Question	Answer	General Principles and Police Powers	Serious Crime and other offences	Property Offences	Sexual Offences	Validation
1	C		▓	▓	▓	▓
2	A	▓	▓		▓	▓
3	B	▓		▓	▓	▓
4	C	▓	▓	▓		▓
5	A	▓		▓	▓	▓
6	B	▓	▓		▓	▓
7	D	▓	▓	▓	▓	
8	A	▓	▓	▓	▓	
9	C	▓		▓	▓	▓
10	D		▓	▓	▓	▓
11	B	▓		▓	▓	▓
12	A		▓	▓	▓	▓
13	D	▓	▓	▓		▓
14	C	▓	▓		▓	▓
15	A	▓	▓	▓		▓
16	B	▓	▓	▓		▓
17	C		▓	▓	▓	▓
18	B	▓	▓	▓	▓	
19	D		▓	▓	▓	▓
20	B	▓		▓	▓	▓
21	A	▓	▓		▓	▓
22	C	▓	▓		▓	▓
23	D	▓		▓	▓	▓
24	B	▓	▓	▓		▓
25	B		▓	▓	▓	▓
26	C	▓		▓	▓	▓
27	A	▓	▓	▓		▓
28	D	▓	▓		▓	▓
29	B	▓	▓		▓	▓
30	C	▓	▓	▓	▓	
Totals		A1	B1	C1	D1	E1

Marking Matrix, Questions 31–60

Question	Answer	General Principles and Police Powers	Serious Crime and other offences	Property Offences	Sexual Offences	Validation
31	B	▓		▓	▓	▓
32	D	▓	▓		▓	▓
33	A		▓	▓	▓	▓
34	C		▓	▓	▓	▓
35	A		▓	▓	▓	▓
36	B	▓	▓	▓	▓	
37	A	▓		▓	▓	▓
38	C	▓		▓	▓	▓
39	D	▓	▓		▓	▓
40	B	▓	▓	▓		▓
41	D		▓	▓	▓	▓
42	C	▓	▓	▓	▓	
43	B		▓	▓	▓	▓
44	B		▓	▓	▓	▓
45	D		▓	▓	▓	▓
46	C	▓	▓	▓		▓
47	D	▓	▓	▓	▓	
48	B		▓	▓	▓	▓
49	D	▓		▓	▓	▓
50	A		▓	▓	▓	▓
51	B	▓	▓		▓	▓
52	D		▓	▓	▓	▓
53	B	▓		▓	▓	▓
54	D		▓	▓	▓	▓
55	C		▓	▓	▓	▓
56	D	▓	▓	▓		▓
57	A	▓		▓	▓	▓
58	B	▓	▓	▓	▓	
59	A		▓	▓	▓	▓
60	A		▓	▓	▓	▓
Totals		A2	B2	C2	D2	E2

Marking Matrix, Questions 61–80

Question	Answer	General Principles and Police Powers	Serious Crime and other offences	Property Offences	Sexual Offences	Validation
61	C	�	▓	▓	▓	
62	A	▓	▓		▓	▓
63	D	▓	▓		▓	▓
64	A		▓	▓	▓	▓
65	B		▓	▓	▓	▓
66	D		▓	▓	▓	▓
67	B		▓	▓	▓	▓
68	C	▓	▓	▓		▓
69	D	▓		▓	▓	▓
70	D		▓	▓	▓	▓
71	A	▓	▓		▓	▓
72	C		▓	▓	▓	▓
73	B	▓	▓		▓	▓
74	D	▓	▓	▓	▓	
75	D	▓	▓	▓		▓
76	B	▓		▓	▓	▓
77	C	▓	▓		▓	▓
78	B	▓		▓	▓	▓
79	A		▓	▓	▓	▓
80	B	▓	▓	▓		▓
Totals		A3	B3	C3	D3	E3

Score Sheet

(Please note that your score for validation questions is not included on this score sheet.)

General Principles and Police Powers	A1		A2		A3		**Total** (out of 27) (= A1 + A2 + A3)	
Serious Crime and other offences	B1		B2		B3		**Total** (out of 17) (= B1 + B2 + B3)	
Property Offences	C1		C2		C3		**Total** (out of 14) (= C1 + C2 + C3)	
Sexual Offences	D1		D2		D3		**Total** (out of 12) (= D1 + D2 + D3)	
						Total questions right (out of 70)	

Questions right	% score	Questions right	% score	Questions right	% score	Questions right	% score	Questions right	% score
1	1.429	15	21.429	29	41.429	43	61.429	57	81.429
2	2.857	16	22.857	30	42.857	44	62.857	58	82.857
3	4.286	17	24.286	31	44.286	45	64.286	59	84.286
4	5.714	18	25.714	32	45.714	46	65.714	60	85.714
5	7.143	19	27.143	33	47.143	47	67.143	61	87.143
6	8.571	20	28.571	34	48.571	48	68.571	62	88.571
7	10	21	30	35	50	49	70	63	90
8	11.429	22	31.429	36	51.429	50	71.429	64	91.429
9	12.857	23	32.857	37	52.857	51	72.857	65	92.857
10	14.286	24	34.286	38	54.286	52	74.286	66	94.286
11	15.714	25	35.714	39	55.714	53	75.714	67	95.714
12	17.143	26	37.143	40	57.143	54	77.143	68	97.143
13	18.571	27	38.571	41	58.571	55	78.571	69	98.571
14	20	28	40	42	60	56	80	70	100

Answer Booklet

1. Answer **C** — The rights may be delayed only for as long as grounds exist and in no case beyond 36 hours after the relevant time as in PACE, s. 41.

Investigators' Manual, para. 1.7.20

2. Answer **A** — B is incorrect as when TRENT first receives the necklace she only has suspicions about the necklace, and does not know or believe it to be stolen and it was a gift so therefore the issue of paying a fair price does not apply. C is incorrect; when she overhears that it is stolen she has already received the goods as a gift. Therefore she does not dishonestly receive the necklace and whether she paid a good price is not the issue as it was a gift. Dishonestly undertakes or assists in their retention, removal, disposal or realisation by or for the benefit of another person, or arranges to do so, does not apply as the benefit is for TRENT not for another person. Therefore when TRENT decides to keep the necklace having found out that it is stolen, TRENT commits theft; making A the correct answer. D is incorrect as she has committed theft and goods obtained by blackmail are property for the purposes of handling.

Investigators' Manual, paras 3.1.1 and 3.7.1

3. Answer **B** — For the offence of making a threat to kill, s. 16 of the Offences Against the Person Act 1861 states:

A person who without lawful excuse makes to another a threat, intending that the other would fear it would be carried out, to kill another or a third person shall be guilty of an offence.

A threat to a pregnant woman in respect of her unborn child is not sufficient if the threat is to kill it before its birth (the unborn child is not a person), making B the correct answer. This makes A incorrect; C is incorrect as the threat can be to the future and D is incorrect as the fear of the victim or third party is irrelevant to the offence—it is the intention of the person making the threat to kill that is the necessary point to prove.

Investigators' Manual, para. 2.7.15

4. Answer **C** — This is not rape as the issue of rape is about consent. In *R* v *B* [2006] EWCA Crim 2945, the Court of Appeal stated that whether an individual had a sexual disease or condition, such as being HIV positive, was not an issue as far as consent was concerned. Therefore as OSBOURNE had clearly consented to sex there was no rape. There is no condition that a person with HIV has to declare their disease or even take precautions. However, if the wearing of a condom was a 'condition' for there to be a sexual act and the offender removed it or did not wear a condom then it would be rape: *Assange* v *Sweden* [2011] EWHC 2489 (Admin).

Investigators' Manual, para. 4.2.3

5. Answer **A** — The Firearms Act 1968, s. 5 states:

(1) A person commits an offence if, without the authority of the Secretary of State or the Scottish Ministers, he has in his possession, or purchases, or acquires, or manufactures sells or transfers [a prohibited weapon].

An electric 'stun gun' has been held to be a prohibited weapon as it discharges an electric current (*Flack* v *Baldry* [1988] 1 WLR 393) and it continues to be such even if it is not working (*Brown* v *DPP* (1992) The Times, 27 March).

This clearly makes A the correct answer.

Investigators' Manual, paras 2.3.4.1 and 2.3.4.2

6. Answer **B** — The Fraud Act 2006, s. 2 states:

(1) A person is in breach of this section if he—
    (a) dishonestly makes a false representation, and
    (b) intends by making the representation—
        (i) to make a gain for himself or another, or
        (ii) to cause loss another or to expose another to the risk of loss.
(2) A representation is false if—
    (a) it is untrue or misleading, and
    (b) the person making it knows that it is or might be untrue or misleading.
(3) 'Representation' means any representation as to fact or as to law, including a representation as to the state of mind of—
    (a) the person making the representation, or
    (b) any other person.

Owing to the fact that this offence is in the *conduct and ulterior intent* of the defendant, the offence is complete when the false representation is made, so is therefore not covered by the Criminal Attempts Act 1981 making C incorrect. Answer A is incorrect as a driving pass certificate is 'other property' and answer D is incorrect as in the case of *Idrees* v *DPP* [2011] EWHC 624 (Admin). When an unidentified imposter presented himself to take a driving test in D's name, it could be inferred that D was complicit in any false representation made by that person with a view to gaining a pass certificate in his name.

Investigators' Manual, para. 3.8.4

7. Answer **D** — The relevant rank for authorisation of directed surveillance is superintendent or above—in ordinary circumstances the authorisation will be for three months (making answers A, B and C incorrect).

Investigators' Manual, para. 1.12.4.2

8. Answer **A** — Section 62 of the Sexual Offences Act 2003 states:

(1) A person commits an offence under this section if he commits any offence with the intention of committing a relevant sexual offence.

Obviously theft is a criminal offence; however, relevant offence under part 1 of the Sexual Offences Act 2003 covers all offences, except it does not extend to other sexual offences under the Protection of Children Act 1978 (the taking of indecent photographs) making A the correct option.

Investigators' Manual, para. 4.7.2

9. Answer **C** — This question is a straight lift from the Manual in relation to manslaughter by unlawful act. The test case is *R v Pagett* (1983) 76 Cr App R 279 (firing a gun at police officers then holding someone else in front of you when officers return fire).

Investigators' Manual, para. 2.1.4.1

10. Answer **D** — An eye-witness may be taken to a particular neighbourhood or place to see whether they can identify the person they saw. It is not necessary for the eye-witness to be accompanied by two officers, making answer C incorrect. Where it is practicable, a record should be made of the eye-witness's description of the suspect before asking the eye-witness to make an identification in such a manner, so rather than being a bar to taking part in a 'street' identification, the first description is a desirable element, making answer A incorrect. Care must be taken not to provide the eye-witness with any information concerning the description of the suspect (if such information is available) and not to direct the eye-witness's attention to any individual unless, taking into account all the circumstances, this cannot be avoided. However, this does not prevent an eye-witness being asked to look carefully at the people standing around at the time or to look towards a group or in a particular direction, if this is necessary to make sure the eye-witness does not overlook a possible suspect simply because they are looking in the opposite direction, making answer B incorrect. Answer D is correct as the officer has complied with the Codes of Practice (Code D, para. 3.2).

Investigators' Manual, paras 1.8.4 to 1.8.4.2

11. Answer **B** — Section 38 of the Offences Against the Person Act 1861 states that whosoever shall assault any person with intent to resist or prevent the lawful apprehension or detainer of himself or of any other person for any offence, commits an offence. The definition tells us that answer D is incorrect as the offence is committed by resisting etc. your own lawful arrest *or* the lawful arrest of *another*, so INGRAM and COLLIER both commit the offence. Once the lawfulness of the arrest is established, the state of mind necessary for the offence is that required for a common assault coupled with an intention to resist/prevent that arrest/detention. It is irrelevant whether or not the person being arrested/detained had actually committed an offence. These principles were set out by the Court of Appeal in a case where the defendant mistakenly believed that the arresting officers had no lawful power to do so. The court held that such a mistaken belief does not provide a defendant with the defence of 'mistake'. Similarly, a belief in one's own innocence, however genuine or honestly held, cannot afford a defence to a charge under s. 38. Therefore, neither man would have a defence in the circumstances described, making answers A and C incorrect and answer B the correct option.

Investigators' Manual, para. 1.4.5

12. Answer **A** — PACE s. 55A allows a person who has been arrested and is in police detention to have an X-ray taken of them or an ultrasound scan to be carried out on them (or both) if:

(a) authorised by an officer of the rank of inspector or above who has reasonable grounds for believing that the detainee:
   (i) may have swallowed a Class A drug; and
   (ii) was in possession of that Class A drug with the intention of supplying it to another or to export; and
(b) the detainee's appropriate consent has been given in writing.

No force can be used.

Making A the correct answer.

Investigators' Manual, para. 1.7.25

13. Answer **D** — For the offence of assault by penetration, s. 2 of the Sexual Offences Act 2003 states:

(1) A person (A) commits an offence if—
   (a) he intentionally penetrates the vagina or anus of another person (B) with a part of his body or anything else,
   (b) the penetration is sexual,
   (c) B does not consent to the penetration, and
   (d) A does not reasonably believe that B consents.

The definition does not include mouth, making B incorrect and A is incorrect as he does commit offences contrary to s. 2. The definition, however, does cover *anything* inserted into the vagina or anus and this does include an animal, meaning that C is incorrect and making D the correct answer.

Investigators' Manual, para. 4.3.1

14. Answer **C** — Under s. 4(2) of the Theft Act 1968 you cannot generally steal land but there are three exceptions.

(1) Trustees or personal representatives or someone in a position of trust to dispose of land belonging to another, can be guilty of stealing it if in such circumstances, they dishonestly dispose of it.

In these circumstances ATKINS is a 'trustee' (he is a director of the company concerned) and has committed the offence, making C the correct answer.

The other exceptions are persons not in possession of the land and actions in certain circumstances of tenants. These should be part of your revision as they are tested frequently in the exam.

Investigators' Manual, para. 3.1.6

15. Answer **A** — The Sexual Offences Act 2003, s. 14 states:

(1) A person commits an offence if—
   (a) he intentionally arranges or facilitates something that he intends to do, intends another to do, or believes another person will do, in any part of the world; and
   (b) doing it will involve the commission of an offence under any of sections 9 to 13.

Sections 9–12 cover offences against children when the offender is over 18. These offences are touching, causing or inciting, sexual activity in the presence of a child, and causing a child to watch a sexual act. Section 13 is a caveat to cover all ss. 9–12 offences when the offender is under 18 years of age. Adrian commits the offence when he facilitates (allows) James and Diane to use a bedroom together knowing that they are having sex. Julie arranges when she books the holiday; sex does not have to have taken place and can be committed in any part of the world. Clearly this makes A correct and B, C, and D incorrect. Section 14 was designed to prevent the sex tourism trade; however, the definition goes beyond that.

Investigators' Manual, para. 4.4.5

16. Answer **B** — In *R (F)* v *DPP* [2013] EWHC 945 (Admin), the High Court examined an application for judicial review of the refusal of the DPP to initiate a prosecution for rape and/or sexual assault on B by A (her former partner). 'Choice' and the 'freedom' to make any particular choice must, the court said, be approached in 'a broad commonsense way'. Against what the court described as the 'essential background' of A's 'sexual dominance' of B and B's 'unenthusiastic acquiescence to his demands', the court considered a specific incident when B consented to sexual intercourse only on the clear understanding that A *would not* ejaculate inside her vagina. B believed that A intended and agreed to withdraw before ejaculation, and A knew and understood that this was the *only basis* on which B was prepared to have sexual intercourse with him. When he deliberately ejaculated inside B, the result, the court said, was B being deprived of choice relating to the crucial feature on which her original consent to sexual intercourse was based and accordingly her consent was negated. Contrary to B's wishes, and knowing that she would not have consented, and did not consent to penetration or the continuation of penetration, if B had had an inkling of A's intention, A deliberately ejaculated within her vagina. This combination of circumstances falls within the statutory definition of rape, making answer A incorrect. There would be no need to consider the presumptions under s. 75 or 76 of the Sexual Offences Act 2003—the specific situations these sections envisage are not represented in this scenario—the only issue of consent to consider is that under s. 74 and it is not present in this situation, making answers C and D incorrect.

Investigators' Manual, paras 4.2.3 to 4.2.4

17. Answer **C** — Answer A is incorrect as the source of the intoxication can be drink or drugs. Intoxication is not a 'general defence' as such—what intoxication does is potentially remove the necessary *mens rea* required for a defendant to commit an offence. Intoxication can be divided into two categories: voluntary intoxication (you got yourself in that condition—MINCHER) and involuntary intoxication (you are not responsible for getting in that condition—DUDLEY). The distinction is important when considering whether the offence alleged is one of 'specific' or 'basic' intent. Where an offence is a specific intent offence, such as murder, defendants who were voluntarily intoxicated at the time the offence was committed may be able to show they were so intoxicated that they were incapable of forming the *mens rea* required for the offence. An individual who is voluntarily intoxicated *would not* be able to say this if accused of an offence of basic intent (MINCHER) as the courts have accepted that a defendant is still capable of forming basic intent even when completely inebriated (*DPP* v *Majewski* [1977] AC 443), making answer D incorrect. Where the offence is a basic intent offence, such as s. 47 assault, defendants who were involuntarily intoxicated (perhaps because their drink had been spiked) at the time of the offence may be able to say that they lacked the *mens rea* for that basic intent offence. So 'intoxication' is relevant as far as DUDLEY is concerned making answer B incorrect. As involuntary intoxication can be raised in answer to a charge of basic intent (s. 47 assault) answer C is correct.

Investigators' Manual, para. 1.4.3

18. Answer **B** — Section 4A of the 1997 Act prohibits a course of conduct relating to the offence of stalking involving fear of violence or serious alarm or distress. Under s. 7(3)(a) of the Act, a 'course of conduct', in the case of a single person, involves conduct on at least two occasions in relation to that person. So although the publication of a fantasy love letter is embarrassing for MASON, that is all it is (making answer A incorrect). When BAYTON sends the email to MASON stating she will kill herself if she sees him with another woman, the two-occasions element of the offence is satisfied.

There are a number of examples of 'stalking' behaviour listed at s. 2A(3) of the Act. The listed behaviours include:

- following a person;
- contacting, or attempting to contact, a person by any means;
- publishing any statement or other material (i) relating or purporting to relate to a person, or (ii) purporting to originate from a person;
- monitoring the use by a person of the internet, email or any other form of electronic communication;
- loitering in any place (whether public or private);
- interfering with any property in the possession of a person;
- watching or spying on a person.

As you can see, BAYTON's behaviour on both occasions would be considered to be 'stalking' behaviour, making answer D incorrect.

The offence under s. 4A can be committed in two ways. The first arm of the offence prohibits a course of conduct that causes the victim to fear, on at least two occasions, *that violence will be used against him/her.* MASON does not fear such violence. However, the second arm of the offence prohibits a course of conduct which causes 'serious alarm or distress' which has a 'substantial adverse effect on the day-to-day activities of the victim'. It is designed to recognise the serious impact that stalking may have on victims, even where an explicit fear of violence is not created by each incident of stalking behaviour. The phrase 'substantial adverse effect on the usual day-to-day activities' is not defined in s. 4A, and thus its construction will be a matter for the courts via judicial interpretation. However, the Home Office considers that evidence of a substantial adverse effect caused by the stalker may include:

- victims changing their routes to work, work patterns or employment;
- victims arranging for friends or family to pick up children from school (to avoid contact with the stalker);
- victims putting in place additional security measures in their home;
- victims moving home;
- physical or mental ill-health;
- victims' deterioration in performance at work due to stress;
- victims stopping or changing the way they socialise.

As BAYTON's course of conduct results in MASON suffering stress and a deterioration in his performance at work, the offence is committed by BAYTON (answer B) which makes answer C incorrect.

Investigators' Manual, para. 2.8.6.2

19. Answer **D** — It is true that any interview of a person under arrest must take place at a police station or other authorised place of detention (answer A and Code C, para. 11.1), however, there are always exceptions. Code C states that if waiting until the interview can be conducted at such a place is likely to:

- lead to interference with or harm to evidence connected with an offence or interference with or physical harm to other people or serious loss of, or damage to property; or
- lead to the alerting of other people suspected of having committed an offence but not yet arrested for it; or
- hinder the recovery of property obtained in consequence of the commission of an offence;

then an interview can go ahead. This makes answer C incorrect as it is not just harm to people that can initiate such an interview. Answer B is also incorrect as no permission from any officer is required.

Investigators' Manual, para. 1.9.3

20. Answer **B** — The Terrorism Act 2000, s. 34(2) states:

(2) A constable who is not of the rank required by subsection (1) may make a designation if he considers it necessary by reason of urgency.
(3) Where a constable makes a designation in reliance on subsection (2) he shall as soon as is reasonably practicable—
   (a) make a written record of the time at which the designation was made, and
   (b) ensure that a police officer of at least the rank of superintendent is informed.

The period of designation begins at the time the order is made and ends on the date specified in the order. The initial designation cannot extend beyond 14 days (s. 35(2)) clearly making B the correct answer.

Investigators' Manual, para. 2.4.7.6

21. Answer **A** — Section 12(1) of the Theft Act 1968 states:

A person shall be guilty of an offence if, without having the consent of the owner or other lawful authority, he takes a conveyance for his own or another's use or knowing that any conveyance has been taken without such authority, drives it or allows himself to be carried in or on it.

A conveyance is taken even if it is put onto another vehicle to do so (*R v Pearce* [1973] Crim LR 321, where a rubber dingy was put on the roof rack of a car and taken away); the dingy was ultimately going to be used as a conveyance by someone in the future, making A the correct answer.

Investigators' Manual, paras 3.6.2 and 3.6.4

22. Answer **C** — The Proceeds of Crime Act 2002, s. 329 states:
A person commits an offence if he—
(a) acquires criminal property;
(b) uses criminal property;
(c) has possession of criminal property.

An additional defence exists under s. 329(2)(c), which states that a person will not commit the offence if he acquired or used or had possession of the property for adequate consideration. The effect of the defence is that persons, such as tradesmen, who are paid for ordinary consumable goods and services in money that comes from crime, are not under any obligation to question the source of the money, making C the correct answer.

Investigators' Manual, para. 3.9.6

23. Answer **D** — The *mens rea* for the offence of assault is the intention or subjectively reckless act which caused the victim to apprehend the immediate infliction of unlawful force. However, words can also negate an assault (*Tuberville* v *Savage* (1669) 1 Mod R3). In this type of assault the defendant is making a *hypothetical* threat and is really saying 'If it weren't for the existence of certain circumstances, I would assault you'. Making D the correct option.

Investigators' Manual, para. 2.7.2.4

24. Answer **B** — The Sexual Offences Act 2003, s. 25 states:

   (1) A person (A) commits an offence if—
      (a) he intentionally touches a person (B),
      (b) the touching is sexual,
      (c) the relation of A to B is within section 27,
      (d) A knows or could reasonably be expected to know that his relation to B is of a description falling within that section, and
      (e) either—
         (i) B is under 18 and A does not reasonably believe that B is 18 or over, or
         (ii) B is under 13.

   Under s. 25 of the Sexual Offences Act 2003 there are offences that apply to blood relatives and those where certain persons have lived in the same household that are not blood relatives until the victim is 18. With these later categories, there are exceptions under s. 27 for this group. Either they were having sex before they became so related; for instance, a step-brother and step-sister who were in a sexual relationship before they became step-brother and step-sister when both 16 or over, or they are legally married in the case of Henry and Jayne, which makes B the correct answer.

Investigators' Manual, para. 4.4.7

25. Answer **B** — When a break is a short one and both the suspect and an interviewer remain in the interview room, the recording media may be stopped. There is no need to remove the recording media and when the interview recommences it shall be recorded on the same audio recording.

Investigators' Manual, para. 1.9.10.6

26. Answer **C** — Section 2(6) of the Modern Slavery Act 2015 states that a person who is a UK national (that includes a British citizen) commits an offence under this section regardless of where the arranging or facilitating takes place, meaning that answer A is incorrect. Answer D is incorrect as the exploitation can take place in any part of the world. The offence under s. 2 of the Modern Slavery Act is committed by arranging or facilitating the travel of another person ('V') with a view to V being exploited. BUCHANAN therefore commits the offence when the arrangements are made (correct answer C), meaning that answer B is incorrect.

Investigators' Manual, para. 2.10.5

27. Answer **A** — The Sexual Offences Act 2003, s. 30 states:

(1) A person (A) commits an offence if—
    (a) he intentionally touches another person,
    (b) the touching is sexual,
    (c) B is unable to refuse because of or for a reason related to a mental disorder, and
    (d) A knows or could reasonably be expected to know that B has a mental disorder and that because of it or for a reason related to it B is likely to be unable to refuse.

Clearly, in these circumstances TENANT was not aware of HANNAH's condition so A is the correct answer. You must also remember that it must be an intentional touching as this can be tested in this section and others within the exam.

Investigators' Manual, para. 4.5.3

28. Answer **D** — The Theft Act 1968, s. 6(2) states:

where a person, having possession or control (lawfully or not) of property belonging to another, parts with the property under a condition as to its return which he may not be able to perform, this (if done for the purposes of his own and without the other's authority) amounts to treating the property as his own . . . regardless of the other's rights.

This makes D the correct answer.

Investigators' Manual, para. 3.1.11

29. Answer **B** — The Fraud Act 2006, s. 11 states:
(1) A person is guilty of an offence under this section if he obtains services for himself or another—
    (a) by a dishonest act, and
    (b) in breach of subsection (2).
(2) A person obtains services in breach of this subsection if—
    (a) they are made available on the basis that that payment has been, is being or will be made for or in respect of them,
    (b) he obtains them without any payment having been made for or in respect of them or without payment having been made in full, and .
    (c) when he obtains them, he knows—
        (i) that they are being made available on the basis described in paragraph (a), or
        (ii) that they might be,

but intends that payment will not be made, or will not be made in full.

When MAY sneaks into the haulage lorry he does not commit the offence under s. 11 because haulage companies do not provide such rides, even for payment. However, he does commit the offence when he obtains the 'service' of a prostitute intending and not paying for the service, making B the correct answer.

Investigators' Manual, para. 3.8.9

30. Answer **C** — The Sexual Offences Act 2003, s. 4 states:

   (1) A person (A) commits an offence if—
      (a) he intentionally causes another person (B) to engage in an activity;
      (b) the activity is sexual;
      (c) B does not consent to the activity; and
      (d) A does not reasonably believe B consents.

   Section 4 is committed when PARSON forces CLARK to masturbate him and forces her to prostitute herself. These are examples from the Keynote area of the Manual and show how important it is to familiarise yourself with the Keynote areas in your preparation for the exam.

Investigators' Manual, para. 4.3.5

31. Answer **B** — The Child Abduction Act 1984, s. 1 states:

   (4) A person does not commit an offence under this section by taking or sending a child out of the United Kingdom without the appropriate consent if—
      (a) he is a person in whose favour there is a child arrangement order in force with respect to the child, and he takes or sends the child out of the United Kingdom for a period of less than one month; or
      (b) he is a special guardian of the child and he takes or sends the child out of the United Kingdom for a period of less than 3 months.

   Therefore B is the correct answer.

Investigators' Manual, para. 2.9.2.2

32. Answer **D** — A person commits an offence if they, without lawful excuse, destroy or damage any property belonging to another intending to destroy or damage any such property or being reckless as to whether any such property will be destroyed or damaged. The case of *R v Fiak* [2005] EWCA Crim 2381 has the same circumstances as this question. The reality was that the blanket could not be used until it had been dried and the flooded cell was out of action until the water had been cleared. Therefore, both had sustained damage for the purposes of the Act. Making D the correct answer.

Investigators' Manual, para. 3.10.2.1

33. Answer **A** — Where a person has been arrested outside England and Wales the relevant time is calculated under s. 41(2)(b) of PACE 1984 and states:

   (b) in the case of a person arrested outside England and Wales, shall be—
      (ii) the time at which that person arrives at the first police station to which he is taken in the force area in England or Wales in which the offence for which is being investigated; or
      (iii) the time 24 hours after the time of that person's entry into England and Wales.

This clearly makes A the correct answer. Relevant time has been tested in the NIE so a good knowledge is important in your preparation.

Investigators' Manual, para. 1.7.16.1

34. Answer **C** — Code B, para. 3.4 states that applications for all search warrants must be made with the written authority of an officer of at least the rank of *inspector* (although in urgent cases where such an officer is not readily available, the most senior officer on duty may authorise the application), making answer A incorrect. Answer B is incorrect as s. 16(3) of PACE states that entry and search under such a warrant must be made within *three* months from the date of its issue. If the warrant is an all premises warrant, no premises which are not specified in it may be entered and searched unless a police officer of at least the rank of *inspector* has, in writing, authorised them to be entered (s. 16(3A)) making answer D incorrect.

Investigators' Manual, para. 1.6.4

35. Answer **A** — It seems that, apart from the offence of murder, attempted murder or treason, the defence is available against any other charge (including hijacking, *R v Abdul-Hussain* [1999] Crim LR 570), making answers C and D incorrect.

The 'serious injury' element relates to the thoughts of the defendant and not to the injury received by the victim, making answer B incorrect. This defence was examined by the Court of Appeal in a case where someone jumped onto the bonnet of the car that the appellant was driving (not too dissimilar from the circumstances of the question). The appellant drove for some distance with the man on the bonnet of the car, braking after a short time to go over a speed ramp. The man fell from the bonnet and the appellant drove on, running the man over and causing him grievous bodily harm. In determining whether or not the defence of 'duress of circumstances' was available, the court held that the jury must ask two questions in relation to the appellant:

- Was he (or might he have been) impelled to act as he did because, as a result of what he reasonably believed, he had good cause to fear he would suffer death or serious injury if he did not do so?
- If so, would a sober person of reasonable firmness and sharing the same characteristics, have responded to the situation in the way that he did?

If each question was answered with a 'yes', the defence would be made out (*R v Cairns* [1999] 2 Cr App R 137).

DRISCOLL did not fear that he would suffer death or serious injury so the defence of duress of circumstances would not be valid.

Investigators' Manual, para. 1.4.7

36. Answer **B** — An STPO can be made and the maximum time this order can be made for is five years initially, making B the correct answer.

Investigators' Manual, para. 2.10.7.4

37. Answer **A** — The offence under s. 4 of the Explosive Substances Act 1883 is committed by a person who makes or knowingly has in his possession or under his control any explosive substance under such circumstances as to give rise to reasonable suspicion that he is not making it or does not have it in his possession or control for a lawful object. 'In your possession' and 'under your control' are widely interpreted—it is not just about having the substance in your immediate possession, making answer D incorrect. Articles which have been held to amount to 'explosive substances' include electronic timers (*R v Berry (No. 3)* [1991] 1 WLR 7 and *R v G* [2009] UKHL 13), making answer B incorrect. The consent of the Attorney General (or Solicitor General) is required before a prosecution can be brought, making answer C incorrect.

Investigators' Manual, paras 2.5.4 to 2.5.4.1

38. Answer **C** — The Firearms Act 1968, s. 17(2) states:

    If a person, at the time of his committing **or** being arrested for an offence specified in schedule 1 to this Act, has in his possession a firearm or imitation firearm, he shall be guilty of an offence under this subsection unless he shows that he had it in his possession for a lawful object.

    Schedule 1 lists many offences but does not include specifically s. 18 wounding, making C the correct answer.

Investigators' Manual, para. 2.3.10.5

39. Answer **D** — The circumstances in which this is committed under s. 12A(2) of the Theft Act 1968 are:

    (a) that the vehicle was driven dangerously on a road or other public place;
    (b) that, owing to the driving of the vehicle, an accident occurred by which injury was caused to any person;
    (c) that, owing to the driving of the vehicle, an accident occurred by which damage was caused to any property, other than the vehicle;
    (d) that damage was caused to the vehicle.

    Damage caused for the original taking of the vehicle is not covered (as at that stage the vehicle concerned has not moved and you do not have the elements of the 'basic' s. 12(1) offence), so therefore the breaking of the window is not included for the offence under s. 12A. There is no need to show any lack of care in driving of the vehicle to prove s. 12A(2)(b), (c) or (d) (*R v Marsh* [1997] 1 Cr App R 67). Therefore D is the correct answer.

Investigators' Manual, para. 3.6.9

40. Answer **B** — Section 13 of the Sexual Offences Act 2003 is an offence created to cover offences 9 to 12 of the Sexual Offences Act 2003 when the offender is under the age of 18 years which lowers the sentence to the like offence of s. 9 from 14 years' imprisonment to 5 years.

    A is incorrect because s. 3 sexual touching would apply when there was no consent by SMYTH. Because SMYTH is aged between 13 years and 16 years, although having consented, it is not true consent therefore it is not s. 3. If WENTWORTH were 18 years old the offence would be s. 9 but because he is under 18 the created offence of s. 13 applies. They would both commit the offence only if they were both under the age of 16 but over the age of 13.

Investigators' Manual, para. 4.4.2

41. Answer **D** — The disclosure provisions of the Criminal Procedure and Investigations Act 1996 set out the retention periods for case material.

Where a person has been convicted, all material which may be relevant must be retained at least until:

- the person is released from custody or discharged from hospital in cases where the court imposes a custodial sentence or hospital order;
- in all other cases, for six months from the date of conviction.

If a person is released from the custodial sentence or discharged from hospital earlier than six months from the date of conviction, material must be retained for at least six months from the date of conviction. Therefore B is incorrect as it cannot be disposed of on release, and furthermore A is incorrect in this regard and with regard to the three months served. C is incorrect not only on lengths but also the fact that custodial sentences and hospital orders do not have different rules. D is therefore correct.

Investigators' Manual, para. 1.11.8

42. Answer **C** — PACE, s. 54A(1) allows a detainee at a police station to be searched or examined or both, to establish:

(a) whether they have any marks, features or injuries that would tend to identify them as a person involved in the commission of an offence and to photograph any identifying marks,
(b) their identity.

A search/examination to find marks under s. 54A(1)(a) may be carried out without the detainee's consent only if authorised by an officer of at least inspector rank when consent has been withheld or it is not practicable to obtain consent. Reasonable force can be used in the exercise of this power.

Investigators' Manual, para. 1.8.6

43. Answer **B** — If it appears that a person does not understand the caution, the person giving it should explain it in his/her own words.

Investigators' Manual, para. 1.9.2

44. Answer **B** — The interviewer shall sign the label and also ask the suspect or any third party present during the interview to sign it. If the suspect or third party refuses to sign the label, an officer of at least the rank of inspector or if not available, the custody officer or, if the suspect has not been arrested, a sergeant shall be called to the interview room and asked to sign it. Making B the correct answer.

Investigators' Manual, para. 1.9.10.10

45. Answer **D** — Section 61A of PACE provides a power for a police officer to take footwear impressions without consent from any person over the age of 10 years who is detained at a police station:

(a) in consequence of being arrested for a recordable offence.

Reasonable force can be used, if necessary to take footwear impressions from a detainee without consent. Therefore D is the correct answer.

Investigators' Manual, para. 1.8.5.3

46. Answer **C** — The Sexual Offences Act 2003, s. 63 states:

(1) A person commits an offence if—
    (a) he is a trespasser on any premises,
    (b) he intends to commit a relevant sexual offence on the premises, and
    (c) he knows that, or is reckless as to whether, he is a trespasser.

This offence is a preparatory sexual offence of intent making A incorrect. The intent to commit a relevant sexual offence can be formed even when already on the premises as a trespasser not necessarily before entry; making D incorrect. A garden is premises for the purposes of s. 63 making B incorrect and C the correct option.

Investigators' Manual, para. 4.7.3

47. Answer **D** — Section 89(2) of the Police Act 1996 states that any person who resists or wilfully obstructs a constable in the execution of his duty, or a person assisting a constable in the execution of his duty, shall be guilty of an offence. Answer A is incorrect as advising a person not to answer questions is not obstructing a police officer (*Green* v *DPP* (1991) 155 JP 816). Answers B and C are incorrect as refusing to answer an officer's questions is not obstruction (*Rice* v *Connolly* [1966] 2 QB 414). Whether that unwillingness to answer is delivered in a polite or rude way does not change anything. If the defendant was under some duty to provide information then that would change the situation but whilst ordinary members of the public have a 'civic' duty to assist the police, they do not have to do so if they do not want to do so. No offence of obstruct police is committed (correct answer D).

Investigators' Manual, para. 2.7.14.3

48. Answer **B** —The issue of transferred *mens rea* can be important in relation to the liability of accessories (in this question POLLOCK is the principal and GUBBIN is the accessory (by counselling the assault)). If POLLOCK's intentions are to be extended to GUBBIN, it must be shown that those intentions were either contemplated and accepted by GUBBIN at the time of the offence, or that they were 'transferred'. There is an excellent example of this in the *Investigators' Manual* which follows the storyline of this question.

EXAMPLE

A person (X) encourages another (Y) to assault Z. Y decides to attack a different person instead. X will not be liable for that assault because it was not contemplated or agreed by X. If, however, in trying to assault Z, Y happens to injure a third person inadvertently, then 'transferred *mens rea*' would result in X being liable for those injuries even though X had no wish for that person to be so injured.

So GUBBIN would not be liable for the assault injuries to EDGE (making answers C and D incorrect). GUBBIN would be liable for the assault injuries to CRANSHAW and BUTTON (correct answer B) making answer A incorrect.

Investigators' Manual, para. 1.1.12

49. Answer **D** — The Public Order Act 1986, s. 18 states:

(1) A person who uses threatening, abusive or insulting words or behaviour, or displays any written material which is threatening, abusive or insulting is guilty of an offence if—
 (a) he intends to stir up racial hatred, or
 (b) having regard to all the circumstances racial hatred is likely to be stirred up.

There is however, a defence under s. 18(4).

In proceedings for an offence under this section it is a defence for the accused to prove that he was inside a dwelling and had no reason to believe that the words or behaviour used, or the written material displayed, would be heard or seen by a person outside that or any other dwelling.

This makes D the correct answer. Sections 18 and 19 of the Public Order Act 1986 have been tested in the exam so some revision is advisable on this subject area.

Investigators' Manual, para. 2.8.2.1

50. Answer **A** — Answer B is incorrect as s. 4 of the Criminal Law 1967 is specified in the Criminal Attempts Act 1981 list of offences that cannot be attempted. Answer C is incorrect as you can attempt an offence that is impossible to commit. Answer D is incorrect as if the offence attempted is triable only on indictment, the attempt will be triable only on indictment. A is correct because even though low-value theft is triable summarily, it is only because of the statutory limit, meaning the offence can still be attempted.

Investigators' Manual, para. 1.3.4

51. Answer **B** — The Theft Act 1968, s. 8 states:

(1) A person is guilty of robbery if he steals, and immediately before or at the time of doing so, and in order to do so, he uses force on any person or puts or seeks to put any person in fear of being then and there subjected to force.

Force does not actually have to be used 'on' the *person*, i.e. on the actual body of the victim. It may be used indirectly, for example on something the victim is carrying and thereby transferring the force to the person: *R v Clouden* [1987] Crim LR 56. Therefore making B the correct answer.

Investigators' Manual, para. 3.2.1

52. Answer **D** — Answer A is incorrect as, for the power under s. 32 to be lawfully used, the officer would have to have reasonable grounds for believing (not suspecting) that the arrested person may present a danger to himself or others. Answer B is incorrect as the officer has a power under s. 32(2)(ii) to search the arrested person for anything which might be evidence relating to *an offence* (not just the offence for which the person was arrested). Answer C is incorrect as PC ARROW can search in PURLEY's mouth (see s. 32(4)). Answer D is the correct answer as trespassing on land with a firearm is a *summary only* offence. Section 32(2)(b) allows an officer to enter and search any premises where the offender was when arrested or immediately before for evidence relating to the offence but only if the offence for which he/she was arrested was *indictable*.

Investigators' Manual, para. 1.6.5.2

53. Answer **B** — The Misuse of Drugs Act 1971, s. 4 states:

(a) to supply or to offer to supply a controlled drug to another in contravention of subsection (1); or

(b) to be concerned in the supplying of such a drug to another in contravention of that subsection; or

(c) to be concerned in the making to another in contravention of that subsection of an offer to supply such a drug.

An offer may be by words or conduct. If it is by words, it must be ascertained whether an offer to supply a controlled drug was made. Whether the accused had a controlled drug in his possession or had access to controlled drugs or whether the substance in his possession was a controlled drug at all is immaterial. Whether the accused intends to carry the offer into effect is irrelevant; the offence is complete upon making of an offer to supply. The offence is committed whether or not the offer is genuine and once the offer is made it cannot be withdrawn.

Investigators' Manual, para. 2.2.4.1

54. Answer **D** — An authorised civilian investigator is allowed to question an arrested person under ss. 36 and 37 of the Criminal Justice and Public Order Act 1994 about facts which may be attributable to the person's participation in an offence. The designated person may also give the suspect the necessary warning about the capacity of a court to draw inferences from a failure to give a satisfactory account in response to questioning.

Investigators' Manual, para. 1.7.3.1

55. Answer **C** — The Bail Act 1976 provides that a surety may notify a constable *in writing* that the accused is unlikely to surrender to custody and for that reason he/she wishes to be relieved of his/her obligations as surety. This written notification provides a constable with the power to arrest the accused without warrant (s. 7(3)).

Investigators' Manual, para. 1.10.7.4

56. Answer **D** — Section 79(8) of the Sexual Offences Act 2003 states that touching includes touching:

- with any part of the body,
- with anything else,
- through anything,

and in particular, touching amounting to penetration (this could include kissing).

The rolling pin constitutes anything and through anything includes massaging FOSTER's back in the first instance through her vest top and bra. This question did not ask when an offence was committed—this is simply 'touching'; make sure you read the question.

Investigators' Manual, para. 4.3.4

57. Answer **A** — It is an offence at common law to take or carry away another person without the consent of that person and without lawful excuse.

A is the correct answer owing to the ruling in *R* v *Hendy-Freegard* [2007] EWCA Crim 1236. When a person moves from place to place '*when unaccompanied by the defendant*' cannot constitute either taking or carrying away or deprivation of liberty, which are necessary elements of the offence. The carrying or taking away takes place when AZIZ throws GRANT into the back of the van.

Investigators' Manual, para. 2.10.2

58. Answer **B** — Section 46 of the Children Act 1989 states:

(1) Where a constable has reasonable cause to believe that a child would otherwise be likely to suffer significant harm, he may—
    (a) remove the child to suitable accommodation and keep him there; or
    (b) take such steps as are reasonable to ensure the child's removal from any hospital, or other place, in which he is then being accommodated is prevented.

A 'child' is someone who is under 18 years old (s. 105), so CATO is classed as a 'child' and answer A is incorrect. The power under s. 46 is split into two parts:

• a power to remove a child to suitable accommodation and keep him/her there; and
• a power to take reasonable steps to *prevent* the child's removal from a hospital or other place.

If PC BUCKINGHAM has reasonable cause to believe that the child would otherwise be likely to suffer serious harm, he may take such steps as are reasonable to prevent CATO from being removed from the hospital (correct answer B). The power under s. 46 does not require the authority of an inspector (answer C is therefore incorrect). It does not allow the removal/ preventing of removal of any person but the child in question, making answer D incorrect.

Investigators' Manual, para. 2.9.4

59. Answer **A** — Where a person is remanded in custody it normally means detention in prison. However, s. 128 of the Magistrates' Courts Act 1980 provides that a magistrates' court may remand a person to police custody:

• for a period not exceeding three clear days (24 hours for persons under 18 (s. 91(5) of the Legal Aid, Sentencing and Punishment of Offenders Act 2012) (s. 128(7));
• for the purpose of enquiries into offences (other than the offence for which he/she appears before the court) (s. 128(8)(a));
• as soon as the need ceases he/she must be brought back before the magistrates (s. 128(8)(b));
• the conditions of detention and periodic review apply as if the person was arrested without warrant on suspicion of having committed an offence (s. 128(8)(c) and (d)).

So FELL could be remanded in police custody for a period not exceeding three clear days and SAYER could be remanded in police custody for a period not exceeding 24 hours, meaning that answers B, C and D are incorrect.

Investigators' Manual, para. 1.10.12

60. Answer **A** — The Serious Crime Act 2007, s. 44 states:

   (1) A person commits an offence if—
      (a) he does an act capable of encouraging or assisting in the commission of an offence; and
      (b) he intends to encourage or assist its commission.
   (2) But he is not to be taken to have intended to encourage or assist the commission of an offence merely because such encouragement or assistance was a foreseeable consequence of his act.

   Section 51 limits the liability of the offence by setting out in statute the exception established in the case *R* v *Tyrrell* [1894] 1 QB 710. Therefore a person cannot be guilty under ss. 44, 45 and 46 of this Act; that is a 'protective' offence, making A the correct answer as FIELD was encouraging an offence that is for her own protection.

   Investigators' Manual, para. 1.3.2

61. Answer **C** — Under the Sexual Offences (Amendment) Act 1992, victims of most sexual offences (including rape, assault by penetration and sexual assault by touching) are entitled to anonymity throughout their lifetime.

   Investigators' Manual, para. 4.1.3

62. Answer **A** — Section 9 of the Theft Act 1968 states:

   (1) A person is guilty of burglary if—
      (a) he enters any building or part of a building as a trespasser and with intent to commit any such offence as is mentioned in subsection (2) below; or...
   (2) The offences referred to in subsection (1)(a) above are offences of stealing anything in the building or part of a building in question, of inflicting on any person therein any grievous bodily harm and of doing unlawful damage to the building or anything therein.

   It would be essential for any s. 9(1)(a) burglary that the person concerned entered as a trespasser. That is not the case for David HOWE as he is entering his own home. If FISHER is entering with David HOWE believing that David HOWE is exercising a lawful right, then FISHER cannot be a trespasser either. Add to this that neither has the intention to steal, inflict grievous bodily harm or commit criminal damage and you would not have a s. 9(1)(a) offence, meaning answer B is incorrect (if both believe there is a legal entitlement to the property then there is no dishonesty and there would be no theft element).

   Section 9 of the Theft Act 1968 states:

   (1) A person is guilty of burglary if—

      . . .

      (b) having entered any building or part of a building as a trespasser he steals or attempts to steal anything in the building or that part of it or inflicts or attempts to inflict on any person therein any grievous bodily harm.

Answer C is incorrect as David HOWE is not a trespasser. David HOWE commits theft when he takes the watch belonging to his wife (making answer D incorrect). However, where the property in question belonged to the defendant's spouse or civil partner, a prosecution for theft may only be instituted against the defendant by or with the consent of the DPP (s. 30(4)). This restriction must also apply to charges of robbery or of burglary by stealing, etc. but does not apply to other persons charged with committing the offence jointly with D; nor does it apply when the parties are separated by judicial decree or order or under no obligation to cohabit (s. 30(4)(a)).

Investigators' Manual, paras 3.4.1 to 3.5.2

63. Answer **D** — Robbery—s. 8 of the Theft Act 1968 states:

A person is guilty of robbery if he steals and immediately before or at the time of doing so, and in order to do so, he uses force on any person or puts or seeks to put any person in fear of being there and then subjected to force.

No robberies are committed. In the offence against CALDERSHAW, the prostitute, the force was not used in order to steal, and in the case of NOWAKOWSKI it was accidental application of force which also does not constitute an offence of robbery.

Investigators' Manual, para. 3.2.1

64. Answer **A** — Section 47ZD of PACE 1984 allows a senior officer (an officer of superintendent rank or above (s. 47ZB(4)(d)) to extend bail from 28 days to three months when certain conditions are met.

Investigators' Manual, para. 1.10.3.2

65. Answer **B** — Group identifications may take place either with the suspect's consent and cooperation or covertly without their consent, making answer A incorrect. Answer C is incorrect as group identifications can involve stationary or moving groups. If it is practicable, then the group identification process will be video recorded but this might not be possible (making answer D incorrect). Group identifications should only take place in police stations for reasons of safety, security or because it is not practicable to hold them elsewhere (correct answer B).

Investigators' Manual, para. 1.8.10

66. Answer **D** — It is worth remembering that where the police officers enter premises *lawfully*, including when they are there by invitation, they are on the premises for *all lawful purposes*. So when they are at 25 Trent Street by invitation they can seize other crime property making A incorrect. If an invitation is terminated, the person needs to communicate that clearly to the officer: it has been held that merely telling officers to 'fuck off' is not necessarily sufficient (*Snook v Mannion* [1982] RTR 321) making B incorrect. C is totally incorrect in these circumstances, making D the correct option.

Investigators' Manual, para. 1.6.1

67. Answer **B** — Actions by the victim will sometimes be significant in the chain of causation, such as where a victim of a sexual assault was injured when jumping from her assailant's car (*R v Roberts* (1971) 56 Cr App R 95). Where such actions take place, the victim's behaviour *will not* necessarily be regarded as introducing a new intervening act. If the victim's actions are those which might reasonably be anticipated from any victim in such a situation, there will be no new and intervening act and the defendant will be responsible for the consequences flowing from them, meaning that answers A, C and D incorrect.

Investigators' Manual, para. 1.2.6

68. Answer **C** — Section 4 of the Sexual Offences Act 2003 (causing sexual activity without consent) states:

(1) A person (A) commits an offence if—
   (a) he intentionally causes another (B) to engage in an activity,
   (b) the activity is sexual,
   (c) B does not consent to engaging in the activity, and
   (d) A does not reasonably believe that B consents.

There is no need to prove sexual gratification, albeit that it may be the case, making answer B incorrect. WEST does not commit any offences as he was unlawfully detained at the time of the offence (evidential presumption under s. 75 of the Act). Therefore C is the correct answer.

Investigators' Manual, para. 4.3.5

69. Answer **D** — The Malicious Communications Act 1988, s. 1 states:

(1) Any person who sends to another person—
   (a) a letter, electronic communication or article of any description which conveys—
      (i) a message which is indecent or grossly offensive;
      (ii) a threat; or
      (iii) information that is false and known or believed to be false by the sender; or
   (b) any article or electronic communication which is, in whole or part, of an indecent or grossly offensive nature.

'Any article' includes dog faeces. This topic does crop up in the NIE so it is worth in your revision taking time to look at it. Note also the defences para. 2.5.4.1—they are very similar to blackmail defences.

Investigators' Manual, para. 2.5.4

70. Answer **D** — A defendant cannot be convicted of statutory conspiracy if the only other party to the agreement is:

- his/her spouse or civil partner;
- a person under 10 years of age;
- the intended victim (s. 2(2) of the Criminal Law Act 1977).

You can conspire to commit offences that are indictable only, triable either way or summary only, making answer A incorrect. Answer B is incorrect as although there must be a 'meeting of minds' for a conspiracy to be committed, the whole purpose of the offence is to catch behaviour leading up to the commission of the offence. Any failure to bring about the end result or abandoning of the agreement will not prevent the offence being committed. The fact that the commission of the offence is impossible as the victim is in Poland will not prevent the offence being committed (s. 1(1)(b)), making answer C incorrect.

Investigators' Manual, para. 1.3.3.1

71. Answer **A** — Robbery is committed when a person steals and immediately before or at the time of doing so, and in order to do so, they use force on any person or put or seek to put any person in fear of being then and there subjected to force. However, there must be a theft for a robbery to occur ('and thief and steal shall be construed accordingly'). If there is no theft, then there is no robbery. Here there is no theft because PUGH honestly believes that he has a lawful right to deprive CANNON of the property. The circumstances of the question are very similar to the case of *R v Robinson* [1977] Crim LR 173, where D, who was owed £7 by P's wife, approached P, brandishing a knife. A fight followed, during which P dropped a £5 note. D picked it up and demanded the remaining £2 owed to him. Allowing D's appeal against a conviction for robbery, the Court of Appeal held that the prosecution had to prove that D was guilty of theft, and that he would not be (under s. 2(1)(a) of the Theft Act 1968) if he believed that he had a right in law to deprive P of the money, even though he knew that he was not entitled to use the knife to get it, i.e. there was no dishonesty. The fact that PUGH knows the means he is using are wrong does not alter the dishonesty element.

Investigators' Manual, para. 3.2.1

72. Answer **C** — The Police and Criminal Evidence Act 1984, s. 18(1) states:

A constable may enter and search any premises **occupied** or **controlled** by a person who is under arrest for an indictable offence, if he has reasonable grounds for suspecting that there is on the premises evidence, other than items subject to legal privilege that relates—

(a) to that offence; or
(b) to some other indictable offence which is connected with or similar to that offence.

I have highlighted 'occupied or controlled' as many persons believe that it states 'owns'. Reasonable suspicion that someone occupies or controls premises is not sufficient, making C the correct option.

Investigators' Manual, para. 1.6.5.3

73. Answer **B** — Answer A is incorrect as the pain-killing drug is a form of property (*R v Bevans* (1987) 87 Cr App R 64). Blackmail is, essentially, an unwarranted demand with menaces, so answer C is incorrect as it does not matter that the menaces of criminal damage were not going to take place 'there and then' (words relevant to robbery and not blackmail). The offence of blackmail is complete at the moment the unwarranted demand with menaces is made and a transfer of property does not need to take place for the offence to be complete, meaning that answer D is incorrect.

Investigators' Manual, paras 3.3.1 to 3.3.4

74. Answer **D** — Section 89(1) of the Police Act 1996 states:

(1) Any person who assaults a constable in the execution of his duty, or a person assisting a constable in the execution of his duty, shall be guilty of an offence.

This offence requires that the officer was acting in the execution of his/her duty when assaulted. If this is not proved, then part of the *actus reus* will be missing. Even a minor, technical and inadvertent act of unlawfulness on the part of the officer will mean that he/she cannot have been acting in the lawful execution of his/her duty. Any action amounting to assault, battery, unlawful arrest or trespass to property takes the officer outside the course of his/her duty (*Davis* v *Lisle* [1936] 2 KB 434). So PC VERRIN would not be acting in the execution of his duty and would not be protected by the law, making answer B incorrect. However, if a prisoner is arrested and brought before a custody officer, that officer is entitled to assume that the arrest has been lawful. Therefore, if the prisoner goes on to assault the custody officer, that assault will be an offence under s. 89(1) even if the original arrest turns out to have been unlawful (*DPP* v *L* [1999] Crim LR 752). This means that answer A is incorrect. The fact that the injuries received by PS BLACKBURN are of a minor nature does not have any bearing on the matter, making answer C incorrect. So the offence has been committed, but only against PS BLACKBURN (correct answer D).

Investigators' Manual, para. 2.7.14.2

75. Answer **D** — The Sexual Offences Act 2003, s. 12 states:

(1) A person aged 18 or over (A) commits an offence if—
    (a) for the purpose of obtaining sexual gratification, he intentionally causes another person (B) to watch a third person engaging in an activity, or to look at an image of any person engaging in an activity,
    (b) the activity is sexual, and
    (c) either—
        (i) B is under 16 and A does not reasonably believe B is 16 or over, or
        (ii) B is under 13.

The issue here is whether NELSON committed the offence and if so at what point was it *first* committed. He knows her to be under 16 and the showing of the images and pictures was for sexual gratification. He can commit the offence by achieving sexual gratification from her watching of the images but, in this question, this was not the case. His motive was to lower the victim's inhibitions. Therefore he commits the offence when he first shows the first image. Image includes a moving or still image and includes an image produced by any means and, where the context permits, a three-dimensional image and it also includes an image of an imaginary person. It does not follow that the sexual gratification has to be immediate, i.e. simultaneous, contemporaneous or synchronised, it can be to put the child in the frame of mind for future sexual abuse (*R* v *Abdullahi* [2006] EWCA Crim 2060), making D the correct answer.

Investigators' Manual, para. 4.4.4

76. Answer **B** — The Criminal Justice and Police Act 2001 makes provision for courts to impose travel restrictions on offenders convicted of drug trafficking offences to prohibit the offender from leaving the United Kingdom at any time during the period beginning from his/her release from custody (other than on bail or temporary release for a fixed period) and up to the end of the order.

The minimum period for such an order is two years (s. 33(3)) where a court:

- has convicted a person of a drug trafficking offence; and
- has determined that a sentence of four years or more is appropriate.

This makes B the correct answer.

Investigators' Manual, para. 2.2.16

77. Answer **C** — The Theft Act 1968, s. 10 states:

A person is guilty of aggravated burglary if he commits any burglary and at the time has with him any firearm or imitation firearm, any weapon of offence, or any explosive.

A is incorrect as although PC HEWITT has formed the intention to steal, this is *after* he entered the house and he *did not* enter as a trespasser. Once he moves into the kitchen (another part of the building) with the intention of stealing, he does enter the kitchen as a trespasser—the intention to steal turns him into one. At this stage we have a s. 9(1)(a) burglary. The defences of lawful authority or reasonable excuse in relation to the possession of an offensive weapon appear not to apply to the offence of aggravated burglary. Therefore, when he enters the kitchen from the hallway he clearly at this point is a trespasser with intent to steal; the items on his utility belt and CS spray make it an aggravated burglary making C the correct answer.

Investigators' Manual, paras 3.5.1 and 3.5.2

78. Answer **B** — There are a number of offences that can be racially or religiously aggravated under the Crime and Disorder Act 1998 but theft and robbery are not included in that list of offences. This makes answers A and C incorrect. Answer C is additionally incorrect as the circumstances described would not amount to an offence of robbery under s. 8 of the Theft Act 1968 (force was used in order to escape and not in order to commit the offence of theft). A s. 39 assault/ battery (under the Criminal Justice Act 1988) *can* be racially or religiously aggravated and although the target of the assault (NASH) is not Jewish the aggravated version of the offence has been committed.

Section 28 of the Crime and Disorder Act 1998 states:

(1) An offence is racially or religiously aggravated for the purposes of sections 29 to 32...if—
   (a) at the time of committing the offence, or immediately before or after doing so, the offender demonstrates towards the victim of the offence hostility based on the victim's membership (or presumed membership) of a racial or religious group; or
   (b) the offence is motivated (wholly or partly) by hostility towards members of a racial or religious group based on their membership of that group.

Clearly CHIVERTON's behaviour when assaulting NASH *demonstrates hostility* towards NASH based on his *presumed* membership of the Jewish faith and Jews are a religious group. This means that answer D is incorrect.

Investigators' Manual, paras 2.6.1 to 2.6.2

79. Answer **A** — The question of admissibility is to be decided by a judge in all cases (making answer B incorrect). Answer C is incorrect as there are a variety of reasons why evidence can be excluded including the incompetence of a witness. Answer D is incorrect as evidence can be excluded under common law as well as elements of PACE 1984.

Investigators' Manual, paras 1.5.1 to 1.5.2.2

80. Answer **B** — It is an offence under s. 33A of the Sexual Offences Act 1956 to keep a brothel, or to manage, or to act or assist in the management of, a brothel to which people resort for the practices of prostitution. For this offence, there must be more than one prostitute (male or female); it is not necessary that full sexual intercourse takes place or even to be offered, making B the correct answer.

Investigators' Manual, para. 4.6.5